D1538045

A Southern Album

A Southern Album

Recollections of some people and places and times gone by

Edited by Irwin Glusker

Narrative by Willie Morris

A & W Visual Library

A Southern Album was developed jointly by
Irwin Glusker and Oxmoor House, Inc.,
Book Division of The Progressive Farmer Company.

Publication under the direction of:

Leslie B. Adams, Jr., *Vice President and Director*

John Logue, *Editor in Chief*

Grace Hodges, *Editor*

Lee Greenwood, *Editorial Assistant*

Project Management by The Glusker Group, Inc.

Irwin Glusker, *Editorial Director*

Laurie Platt Winfrey, *Chief of Picture Research*

Sam Ehrlich, *Picture Source Bibliographer*

Christian von Rosenvinge, *Layout*

Carl K. K. Lau, *Layout Assistant*

...**Who are you** who will read these words and study these photographs, and through what cause, by what chance, and for what purpose, and by what right do you qualify to, and what will you do about it; and the question, Why we make this book, and set it at large, and by what right, and for what purpose, and to what good end, or none: the whole memory of the South in its six-thousand-mile parade and flowering outlay of the façades of cities, and of the eyes in the streets of towns, and of hotels, and of the trembling heat, and of the wide wild opening of the tragic land, wearing the trapped frail flowers of its garden of faces; the fleet flush and flower and fainting of the human crop it raises ...those, each, whose lives we knew and whom we love and intend well toward, and of whose living we know little in some while now, save that quite steadily, in not much possible change for better or much worse, mute, innocent, helpless and incorporate among that small-moted and inestimable swarm and pollen stream and fleet of single, irreparable, unrepeatable existences, they are led, gently, quite steadily, quite without mercy, each a little farther toward the washing and the wailing, the sunday suit and the prettiest dress, the pine box, and the closed clay room whose frailly decorated roof, until rain has taken it flat into oblivion, wears the shape of a ritual scar and of an inverted boat: curious, obscene, terrifying, beyond all search of dream unanswerable, those problems which stand thickly forth like light from all matter, triviality, chance, intention, and record in the body, of being, of truth, of conscience, of hope, of hatred, of beauty, of indignation, of guilt, of betrayal, of innocence, of forgiveness, of vengeance, of guardianship, of an indenominable fate, predicament, destination, and God.

—James Agee, from *Let Us Now Praise Famous Men*

My Own Private Album

The Burden and Resonance of My Memory

By Willie Morris

Part I   *When I was a boy growing up on the banks of the Yazoo, I would lie on the ground in August lassitude and frame my hands to look at the sky and the clouds, as if I were making a painting, or a photograph, out of what I saw. One day I got a kite hundreds of feet into the sky, the highest I had ever managed with a kite, and then I lay back and watched it rise and fall, as a jackdaw knifes with the wind, the string tugging gently in my hand to remind me that what I had done was mine. All about me were the green and lazy sights of summer, and as I spied the kite so far away, reaching, it seemed, to the clouds, I felt I was playing a lonesome game with time itself, with the slow, dreamy drifting of time as it hovers and stands still, pausing briefly on its journey before it passes and goes away.*

I am a Southerner. I like the feel of these words. I could no more be otherwise than I could shed my outer skin or change the color of my eyes. I know, because I have thought about it.

As a young man I professed a shame for my origins, told myself I sprang from a cursed inheritance. Going far away pitched me off-stride, as the distance runner might lose his balance before regaining it for the long road ahead. Whether we are black or white: it happens in those years to some of us, but unless we are fools and seek more than we bargain for, we always come back to what we are, because what we are has behind us the force of all simple revelations: we are different.

"Tell me about where you come from," a friend once said to me, and I could do no better than this:

I love the South because it helps me remember. It helps me know who I am. When I am there, it haunts me that all my people—my great-grandparents, my grandfather and grandmother, my aunts and uncles, my father—lie close by in the dark earth. *Be with me,* my father whispered to me when he was dying. I am aware that I am among them and that they will always be with me.

One day, alone in a hotel in Jackson, waiting through an afternoon of rain and high winds for an airplane that would take me East, I was overcome with the sudden recognition that all my people who settled and nurtured and then led this state and begot and suffered its worst calamities are buried under broken tombstones on a ruined, forgotten hill ten miles away. In the lonely wait before a journey I had made a dozen times, the spirit of them, the brevity of their days, the monumental retribution which settled at last upon their years on earth, taunted me beyond the bearing. I felt I should go out to the hill, if only to pay obeisance to the elemental truth that I knew who they were, sensed something of what their lives must have been, acknowledged my flesh as theirs. In that moment I knew for the first time that a man could love his past and be in misery with it.

Could my generation be the last to have known, and lived, the old warring impulses to be both Southern and American? Before the great television culture, before *Brown v. Board of Education,* before the federal expressways and suburban sprawls which so disfigured and reshaped the land we had once known, the South of my youth was more closely akin, physically and in spirit, to the 1920s and 1930s than to the 1960s and 1970s. In its driftlessness and isolation and vanity it was a pause, a halfway point; it had a patina of time, as poignant and fragile as an old photograph. Why, in an age of Auschwitz and Hiroshima and Indochina, with the whole modern experience of the human race in such regimented suffering and rapine, did this South deign to endure, to remain an entity, or an essence, which somehow profoundly mattered unto itself? It endured because of its human beings: its black people, its white people, its politicians, its characters, its writers. For history is not events, as J. Bronowski reminded us—it is people acting and living their past in the present: the uniqueness of man, the pride in his gifts, his genius for flexibility and improvisation. Unexpressed in the marrow of the South, even in seeming, tragic contradiction, was the elegy in Agee's words: "In every child who is born, under no matter what circumstances, and of no matter what parents, the potentiality of the human race is born again."

Are the South's people not now as important as its things? I cannot begin to answer. But in the blood of me I know its single most enduring quality has been the burden of its memory, its past of anguish and despair and cruelty but also of rare courage and honor and sacrifice; from its common sense of soil sprang the disposition in the soul of it for the most intense strivings, triumphs, and defeats, for imagination and exuberance and playfulness, for the venerable and familiar punctuations of life's continuity. All this was enough to make the South the most distinctive part of America, and its people the most distinctive Americans. It would embrace the extreme of the American dream even in its act of denial, and since it was forever the crucible of the national guilt, the playing-ground for all the nation's oscillations of idealism and idealism's retrenchments, it was driven back upon itself into its own ambivalence.

This alone was enough to implant in its sons, no matter where they would live, a remembrance of community.

Cemeteries

A wonderful Friday afternoon in springtime during the war. We gather in the graveyard after school. Far below us the town lies drowsily in the sunshine. The spring rains have washed away most of a bluff; we see something which horrifies and titillates us. The gravediggers have exhumed several coffins to keep them from washing away, then buried the coffins farther up a desolate hill. Gleaning and gathering like squirrels, we muster our courage to look down into the open graves, dark and fetid, and after a while we jump into one of them, enjoying the blood-rushing terror. It is good to be alive in the Mississippi spring and to play around like this in old graves.

The Episcopal Cemetery, Alexandria, Virginia, a Fourth of July afternoon: I tell my son to look for his great-great-great-great-grandmother.

We part in our quest. Nearby a Negro cabdriver in an air-conditioned taxi awaits us.

A long silence. Then, from far away, "Dad! I found her." I walk to where he is. The two of us contemplate her:

Sara Harper
Born 1775   Died 1800

"Twenty-five years old," he says at last.
"That's not much, is it?"
"Where's her husband?"
"He went on down to Mississippi."
"You mean, just left her and went?"

"I suppose so."

"But Mississippi's so far away!"

The Vicksburg National Cemetery. A brisk March morning in 1968. We have come here with a well-known New York editor, and now we are standing at the top of the bluffs among all the boys who died a hundred and five years before for Pemberton and Grant. Many of the stones are inscribed only with numbers.

On this high ground, when I was fourteen, I once stood with my trumpet waiting to play echo to taps for the boys of the Dixie Division brought home from Korea. The plaque is still there among the stones, the words which leapt out to me then like living things, filling me with an excitement and a sorrow I could not comprehend: *Fourscore and seven years ago our fathers brought forth on this continent....* Down below, far beyond the battlefield tableau, the cannon and statues and thousands of white crosses, was the river, brown and lonesome and seeming to move hardly at all.

There are four of us, of our four generations, accompanying the New York editor. My grandmother, the last of hers, called Mamie, ninety years old now, born the year the Northern troops withdrew from Mississippi—grandniece of the first territorial governor, niece of another governor and United States senator—repository of those vanished times for me. The fifteenth time she saw *Gone With The Wind,* she told me when I was a boy, she went to look at the furniture. With her there: my mother, sixty-eight; myself, thirty-two; my son, seven. There aren't many of us left.

Halfway down the hill, among the dead of Illinois, the New Yorker asks, with a benign smile, "Mamie, do you think all these boys died in vain?"

Another generation—my mother—interrupts. "Why ask her that?"

"Mamie knows more than we do," I suggest.

"Oh, son," Mamie says, gazing very far away, out toward the river, toward the green bluffs of Louisiana. "I don't know. I don't think so."

"Well," my mother replies, "They'd all be dead and buried now anyway."

There is a photograph I saw in the library when I was a boy: crowds of men, women, children, dogs gathered in celebration about the town's Confederate monument at its dedication. In the background are dozens of horse-drawn wagons, and on a platform near the monument there is a speaker in full rhetorical motion. And at the top of this edifice is a bronze soldier with hands extended, poised there to accept a flag and a rifle from a lady.

I looked closely at the figures there: little girls in crinoline dresses, women with parasols, men in top hats smoking cigars. I looked at this for the longest time, until an obscure silhouette at the corner of my eye caught my attention: at the fringes of the crowd, all by himself, a small Negro boy, barefoot and in a straw hat, watching the scene.

On his face in repose is a look of expectancy, almost of mournful innocence, as if he is waiting for someone to tell him something he does not know. Who is he? What became of him? I left the library and went to the monument, touched its surfaces with my hand, looked around me at the empty knoll where all the people had been.

The last of the great, desultory Southern drivers

One of life's pleasures was driving over long Southern distances—unending summer afternoons with Katie Culpepper, who attended the baton-twirling clinics at Ole Miss two weeks every year; spinning about the country roads of the Delta, past flat green plantations where Negroes chopped cotton in the fields, slowly standing erect when the car came past, ghosts, in sunlight, frozen figures eyeing us from afar. The bayous running like veins through the rich alluvial land. Crossroads groceries with medicine posters on their walls and barns with faded Bull Durham signs. Men on their haunches, spitting tobacco in the dust, boys standing barefoot by unpainted churches, mean and beseeching. The feed stores, seed stores, and courthouse squares of other towns smaller than our own. Drinking cold Jax and tossing the empty cans into the back seat. All of a sudden Katie singing:

> When it's dark-ness on the Del-ta,
> That's the time my heart is light,
> When it's dark-ness on the Del-ta,
> Let me lin-ger in the shelter of the night.

On the radio, from the local station, testimonials to Tally-Ho, curative of aches, blues, and constipation. In the backroom of his father's drug store in Belzoni, our friend from rival teams, mixing liquid in washtubs with a broomstick:

"Tab!"

"Hey, now! Come on in, you heah?"

"What you doin', Tab?"

"Can't you see? Makin' this week's Tally-Ho."

In college, on any whim, driving a black-and-white Chevy with dual exhausts hundreds of miles into the nighttime, up to Memphis or down to the Gulf, watching an autumn moon above the sea of dead stalks, the bare trees silhouetted against a sweep of skyline. Once we drove all the way to New Orleans without a stop for Saturday night in the Quarter, then turned around and came back, and the next week drove up to Asheville to see Thomas Wolfe's grave with the angel on the tomb, where the caretaker said: "Tom Wolfe never amounted to much."

Never failing to stop for hitchhikers when the mood was right—wandering Negroes and soldiers and dirt farmers; one learned a great deal about America from these meanderers of the Southern night: the passions that sweep across it, its loneliness, its jubilations and uncertainties. One developed a mystic longing for the Southland in these journeys, the things which came to me from what I felt of its history were acutely visual: Jefferson dwelling on governance in the gardens of Monticello, Lincoln striding the doomed streets of Richmond with a ragtail bodyguard wary of snipers, Lee in nightfalls after the war riding Traveller over the gutted land of old battlefields, all the years of politicians and preachers prancing the countryside.

But mostly it was solitary driving. I loved to see some unfamiliar stretch of road unfold before me in the darkness and the sleepy little towns of the Southland slip by me and the splattering of the insects on the windshield. I would look at the darkened houses along empty streets and wonder who lived in them and what kind of people they might be; moving on through the night, I felt I was collecting secrets about these lonesome places that no one outside the neighborhood could ever know. The empty road was the best of it, and I would keep the speedometer precisely at 70, wheel-straddling the dead dogs, cats, rabbits, and snakes, rolling on toward nowhere. On the radio, the gospel singing from Del Rio, the nocturnal preachers pledging damnation from Piedras Negras, the love tunes of the fifties from the Blue Room of the Roosevelt Hotel on WWL in New Orleans, all those mindless tunes which embraced my generation with their poignant desire and, for all I know, shaped us into what we are. This was before the expressways arrived in such numbers, bypassing the little towns and encouraging them to die, hastening the migrations to the swollen new cities of the South. There is no doubt that we were the last of the great, desultory Southern drivers.

Violence

Societies are shaped by the land from which they emerge. This land was unremitting, retrieved from its brutal swamps by men of all colors and gradations known to the species, fighting it into its tentative submission, a land fraught with deceits and nobilities.

The place where I grew up was violent. I absorbed violence in the church and on the playing fields. The elements were violent: savage, unpredictable seasons, deep rainfalls, wild winds and thunders. Violence was in the memory of my people. "Everything, weather, all, hangs on too long. Like our rivers, our land: opaque, slow, violent; shaping and creating the life of man in its implacable and brooding image."* I have a white boy's recurring awareness of this hovering violence, isolated acts as senseless now in memory as they had been when they happened: white against black, black against white, whites and blacks against their own. An image remains, etched as starkly as a woodcut: across from the bus station, a concrete banister where Negroes sit waiting for the bus. We turn the corner with screeching tires, the driver opens the door and drives close to the curb; we look behind us as the Negroes topple backward off the banisterlike dominoes.

*(Faulkner, *As I Lay Dying.*)

Where did we learn to do this? What put it in our bones? In time one learns the truly gentle person is the one who has warred against his own violence. Some of the gentlest people are Southerners and, perhaps, some of the meanest: the extraordinary apposition of civility and violence.

Textures of boyhood

The floods in spring, the muddy waters overflowing into the streets of town, and then the open trucks with the convicts in back on their way to the levees, their black-and-white stripes somber under the purple skies.

The Negro church set among the chinaberries at the foot of the hills; stealing on tiptoe into a back pew, looking around there at all the gradations of colors and wondering for the first time if we might not be *related.*

The swamp woods where my father took me, he with a .12-gauge, I trailing behind with my .22, watching the marks of his boots behind him filling with the blackish water. Mosquitoes descending in flurries in the gloomy hardwood forest, trees festooned with vines and creeping plants; cold silence, the sun opening suddenly in a palmettoed clearing, and giant spiderwebs shimmering in the eerie light.

Summers of wisteria. Families on porches in the hot, still nights, exchanging hellos with everyone who walked past. The broad lawns wet with a summer's dew, the lightning bugs glowing and vanishing as far as the eye can see, and the night alive with the chirping and rustling of small Delta things.

A river not to be tampered with: the way it opened up and wound around; the ruined houses along its banks; the moss hanging over it from the bright willows and cypresses, bent down like wise men trying to tell us something; visions of the heroic Ironclad floating down from the shipyard at the bend to terrorize the Yankee armada at Vicksburg. Throwing rocks at the turtles, shooting BBs at empty bottles, then climbing high into the cypresses to watch the fishermen drift by.

Classes in history. The rights of states. Miss Red Hester poised over her books. Shiloh, the Wilderness, Old Cold Harbor. Figures from the Civil War, like ghosts.

Children of the poor from Graball Hill, coming to school barefoot in rough khaki or denim, crossing over to the grocery store at noon for a candy bar and a glass of water.

Political rallies in the back country, the barbeque and corn-on-the-cob and yams being served up from long wooden tables in a world of flies. The preachers bless the politicians, and the Negroes standing in the back among themselves laugh in wild chorus at the denunciations heaped torrentially upon them.

A photograph wrapped in tissue: The Mississippi Legislature, 1875. The faded likeness of my great-grandfather, surrounded by black faces of Reconstruction.

Baseball games on backwoods fields, sitting behind a chicken-wire backstop for the best view of the action. From a portable radio comes a magic game out of Yankee Stadium: the sounds of the two games, our own and the one from New York, merge and roll across the bumpy outfield beyond the red gullies into the woods.

Interracial football games in Lintonia Park: first black against white, then intermingled —shaking our heads in rhythm, strutting from huddles with limbs swinging—until one day the police came by and made us break it up.

The cool serenity of the Dixie Theater; forsaking it finally for the afternoon's sun, the stark sunlight destroying in the instant one's grandest absorptions: Bacall, Dahl, Roman, Mayo. Then down the bereft summer street, with old men under the awnings whittling wood, to Carr's Drug Store for a vanilla coke, gazing in scarcely concealed displeasure at the dyspeptic country girl behind the counter, no Bacall, until she asks, "What's wrong with you, anyhow?"

Leaves falling on smoky Indian summer afternoons, the air crisp and the sound of dogs barking, the echo of an axe on wood and of train whistles far away. Truckloads of raw cotton coming in for ginning, and along every street and road the dirty white bolls have fallen to the earth.

The town viewed from the kudzu hills: a bare and forlorn business district; low-roofed brick stores, gins, loading platforms; the Negro shacks on stilts in the bottoms; the cotton stretching all the way to the houses on the white residential streets lined with elms and water oaks; the sudden emergence of the fields from shade into open country bright with bolls. Farther out on the dark flat land, the old plantation house made of cypress boards with its screened gallery and square-cut columns and cross hall and kitchen ell; the message written in plaster by the Northern soldiers who quartered there: "To the owner of this house. Your case is a hard one and I pity you."

Part II   *Now I live far away, at an easternmost littoral of America. In an early dusk of winter I ask, Who am I? What am I doing here?*

There is an old Negro man out here whom we all know, who wanders around town at all hours, drinking cheap wine behind hedges and trees, talking incessantly to himself, head aslant in his aimless journey. No one knows where he sleeps, if he does at all. I am told that he came here years ago to work on the potato farms, and that he could do the labor of three men. Now eight or ten times a day I see him, one moment down on the turnpike to Sag Harbor, five minutes later in the graveyard with its memorial to the boy who died at Antietam, then in front of the church where Mrs. Stowe's father preached his sermons, and I have even sighted him as far away as the dunes and the ocean. Once my son and I, waiting for the train, saw him emerge from a diaphanous fog like a specter, shuffling down the middle of the tracks. Being a Southern boy, I must believe he is a reminder to the town of something it does not truly know of itself, but many here would not understand what I mean.

It is a very small town here in the winter, and much as the potato fields remind me of early cotton, the village brings back something of my hometown to me. Along the streets, in daylight and darkness, there are the sounds of black voices, all the vanished echoes of my youth. Small Negro children wander about the streets in swarms as they did in my town, and on Saturdays their parents sit on the front porches along the turnpike and socialize with high laughter and chatter. The population is nearly half black, most of them Southerners, and one of the sadnesses of the town is that it does not have the tragedy of remembrance. Does it not lack the shared past, the common inheritance in the land, which helped the South survive? A generation ago the farmers brought the Negroes out here and then spurned them.

Last Christmas we were opening presents. I remember the whip of the wind in frozen branches and the rattle of fallen leaves. We were sitting in front of the fire when we saw the old Negro man outside. My son ran out to give him a present in a bottle.

Often when I was out of sorts I would go home, back to the South—driving out of Manhattan at nightfall, following the big diesels on the great eastern turnpikes. Down the wastes of New Jersey into Delaware and Maryland, past the monuments of Washington which beckoned like trusted companions in the surrounding darkness, on through the battlefield country of the Rapidan and the Rappahannock, the tobacco fields, and the Dismal Swamp, the Carolinas, then skirting the mighty skyline of Atlanta, the red hills of Alabama, and across the line into Mr. Bill Faulkner's country.

But as I get older, this becomes more difficult. I suffer the familiar places, associate far too painfully with old happenings, griefs, and joys. Houses, streetcorners, stretches of countryside bring back to me in a dreadful rush all the things that happened to me there; I see home in a dreamlike vision, seeing it the way it was a quarter of a century ago. I remember too much.

I have the memory of going home from college on holiday weekends in the spring. Half of Texas and the upper boot of Louisiana fell behind me, and in the drive through the languid hills above Natchez with the blossoming dogwoods and jonquils and burning bushes, I knew when I reached my destination all would be as I expected it to be, so that sometimes I made the trip last a little longer to savor the tenderness of coming back to that one place where the contours of old, tangible things were so commensurate with the orderly longings of one's life. When I was a boy I would see the people in big cars with Northern plates stop on the main street to stretch their legs and look about at the lonesome façades before going somewhere to drink coffee or empty their bladders, but I never felt I was returning from college to one of those lost little places of Dixie. The place which awaited me on those weekends was more than my home, it was the sanctuary of my innocence. Every house went by its family name; it seemed I knew every tree. And when I descended the last hill and all of it was stretched out for me in a morning's mist, I sensed that voices, movements, the very commerce of living had rested in suspension while I was away and now, condiments to a virginal conceit, would resume for me all over again. Hope, pleasure, order—on those rides home they reaffirmed the same emotion: the emotion of belonging serenely to the Lord's good earth.

An evening at one of the colleges in New England, a ferry's ride across Long Island Sound. I am with two respected writers, Southerners, who teach here. In a gracious study lined with books, students are asking questions.

"I've been listening closely," one of them says, "and I have this to ask. How can three such civilized men come from such a barbaric region?"

These words are addressed to me. On a question of such import, I say, I must defer to my distinguished elder, Mr. Robert Penn Warren.

Red Warren, of Guthrie, Kentucky, looks into his bourbon, rattles the ice gently in his glass. "I'm a little tired of that question," he says, finally, then after a tender silence, "I suppose my answer is, it has to do with inoculation against hookworm."

An interview on television with a young Negro congressman, a protégé of Dr. King's, a leader of the Movement, from Georgia.

The interviewer is an exceedingly tough New York girl. In a brisk chronology, she outlines the dire failings of his part of the world. She does not comprehend, she says, why human beings with black skin can live here. She is relentless against all evil.

The young congressman will have none of it. He is also a preacher—savvy, cool, a teller of stories, touched with easy laughter and the rhythms of the Bible. When he was coming up, he says, he had white friends—he has a lot more now. There is a relaxed feeling of community here, he suggests to her. Problems, most certainly, problems aplenty—but hope, too, always hope.

She persists. A frown creases his forehead; he does not want to be rude to this well-intentioned visitor: "But I'd rather live here than where you live," he says. Now she is incredulous. "Why?" she asks.

"Because we have *relationships* here," he replies. "We know one another. Why, up there, it doesn't matter whether you're black *or* white. People just don't pay attention to people." Then he laughs. He has a sense of who he is.

A photograph from my hometown newspaper: The football team from my old high school poses on the same turf where we had our tenacious struggles twenty-five years ago. There are eighteen black boys, eighteen white. They are still called the Yazoo Indians.

Now I am watching the college football game on national television, in a fisherman's bar only a stone's throw from the Atlantic. Playing are the University of Mississippi and the University of Alabama in the big stadium in Jackson, just down the street from the hospital where I was born.

The spectators wave hundreds of Confederate flags; the Ole Miss band plays *Dixie* every four or five minutes; the air is vibrant with rebel yells. Down on the field the two teams, each of them about half black and half white, exchange soul-slaps when something notable happens for their cause; the black and white cheerleaders and drum majorettes strut and cartwheel along the gridiron. A Negro halfback for the Ole Miss Rebels breaks free for a long touchdown. His white teammates embrace him joyously, and the band plays *Dixie* for the fiftieth time.

"How ungenerously in later life we disclaim the virtuous moods of our youth," Evelyn Waugh wrote in *Brideshead Revisited,* "living in retrospect long summer days of unreflecting dissipation, Dresden figures of pastoral gaiety. Our wisdom, we prefer to think, is of our own gathering, while, if the truth be told, it is most of it, the last coin of a legacy that dwindles with time."

The theme of this album is memory. There are certain moments in one's lifetime, moments which elicit some deep interior tension and seem to mirror all the longings and intuitions of one's existence. There are not many of these moments, and they always come without warning, instantaneous in their enactment, yet with the passing of the days they become life's signposts: they are the substance of memory.

I remember one such moment, on the balcony of a villa in Haiti, in a Sunday twilight of three years ago.

I had been in Port-au-Prince three weeks. I had fallen in love with this mournful, extravagant country—the way the people moved along its roadways, its raw exteriors, its passionate colors. It, too, was home.

I was looking at houses to rent for the following summer, and on a steep hillside I found one I liked. I walked out alone on the central balcony. It was that enchanted time just before dusk when all the colors of the tropical day blend for a transitory instant into the deepest shades of orange and purple. Behind me the grey clouds loomed over Kenscoff. I looked down at the cathedral and the palace and beyond these to the harbor. From far below the hillside in the direction of the water I became aware of a vast murmur of hundreds of voices: chants and shouts echoed back to me across the primitive village facades, and from a loudspeaker—in his native Creole language—a Protestant preacher was unmistakably exhorting his flock to salvation. A brief silence, invaded only by the muted human rustlings of that ancient city, and then, again in that tragic tongue, the voices lifted into the hymn of my Mississippi childhood:

Abide with me
Fast falls the eventide
The darkness deepens
Lord, with me abide…

I have since thought often of all the failures we are doomed to bear, of that symbiosis of ecstasy and suffering which is the burden of all mortals, but the sound of these words in the twilight turned something in me, seemed to touch the sinews of my life.

"The past is never dead," Faulkner said. "It's not even past."

I have not been home in a long time. Then it was for Mamie's funeral.

She was one of the handful of people I loved who even now seem ageless and set apart. I was nourished in the echoes of her laughter. She was my favorite human being. I always pictured her as a little girl, barefoot and in a cotton dress, or watching the trains to Jackson or Vicksburg on the arched bridge where my grandfather one day proposed to her, or hiding half a dozen Negro men in a deserted chicken shed after a race riot which erupted during a political barbeque. There was not much formal education for girls there then, and her older sisters never found husbands because there were no men. But there was a touch of nobility in her generation of Southern women, for they emerged from suffering, and they moved through life imbued with the tenacity of the Scriptures.

When I was a boy, she and I took long walks around town in the gold summer dusk, out to the cemetery or for miles and miles to the Old Ladies' Home, talking in torrents between the long silences. All about us were forests of crepe myrtles and old houses faintly ruined. Widow ladies and spinsters sat on the galleries cooling themselves with paper fans from the funeral home, and we greeted each lady by turn, and then Mamie told me who they were and what had happened to their people; sometimes I would make my rounds of them alone, drinking iced tea heavy with mint leaves, suffusing myself in their strange, childlike voices. We must have made an unlikely pair on these long ago journeys, Mamie in her flowing dress and straw hat, I in a T-shirt and blue jeans with a sailor's cap on my head, separated by our sixty years. Only when I grew older did I comprehend that the years between us brought us together. *What are hills? How old are horses? Where do people go when they die?* She always tried to answer me, but mostly she told me stories. One autumn twilight she sighted a beautiful white pebble and she told me she had found it down by the town well when she was ten years old.

In the funeral home she lay in the front room. I looked and listened, as a man will when he comes home. I watched my son looking furtively from time to time in her direction. It was his first funeral. He is a Manhattan boy, and he lurked now in corners watching the whole town come through. "He looks just like you did," they said. "He favors you." They admired his Yankee accent.

The night she died there was a wreck—five teen-age boys drag racing in two cars on the highway in a rainfall—a frightful collision. People talked of it: twelve hours to get one boy out of the wreckage, limbs and faces shorn apart, closed coffins with photographs on the lids. At the top of the hill the country people came to see the wrecked cars. They stuck their heads in the shattered windows to see the blood on the seats, a bloodied pair of glasses on a floorboard. Long lines formed, and the eyes of the beholders were glazed.

"To have been ninety-seven," the preacher said. "But to have been sixteen."

"There's never been a tragedy here like this," a newcomer said to me. I was standing with an old friend, the editor of the paper. We did not need words to remind ourselves of the Negro cotton-pickers hurled headlong out of a truck into a pecan tree a quarter of a century ago; of the Illinois Central freight that demolished the school bus in 1953; of a few random murders; or of all the boys lost over the years to the Yazoo River— death every day, death everlasting, among people who have lived in such proximity amidst the familiar landmarks and places, punctuated by the immemorial changes of the seasons.

Now when the boy goes into the village with our labrador, Ichabod H. Crane, he wears in his belt his great-great-grandfather's sword. My grandmother gave it to me when I was his age, and one day, my intuition telling me it was time, I gave it to him. The ceremony was scant.

"Your great-great-grandfather had whiskers and chewed tobacco," I said. "He read Greek and was editor of a newspaper. After the Civil War he took to dirt farming with one mule. He lived to be seventy-five and had nine sons and seven daughters."

"Where is he now?"

"He's buried back home. Remember your great-grandmother's funeral? He was her father."

"Did this sword kill anybody?"

"I don't know."

He looked at it for a long time, then took it in his hand. "Thank you, Dad."

Now, trailed as ever by his dog, he is pirouetting on the lawn with the sword. The English beech is faded to copper and half-stripped of its leaves, the waters of our pond mirror the gold and russet of the trees— all around the boy and the dog are the memorials to the island's dying autumn, from the ocean there is a nip of the early northern winter in the air, and I watch from the window while he stands motionless on the dense carpet of leaves. As the sunshine catches the sheen of Major Harper's sword, he and the dog are looking up into the beech tree, at a grey squirrel playing among the branches; the two of them are caught for me in this brief frieze, two small creatures under a moody sky, and without knowing it I am framing them with my hands, trying to capture them in my mind's eye as they touch me in that instant in my heart.

William Faulkner,
Lafayette County, Mississippi, 1962

I Decline to Accept the End of Man

I decline to accept the end of man. It is easy enough
to say that man is immortal simply because he will
endure: that when the last ding-dong of doom has
clanged and faded from the last worthless rock
hanging tideless in the last red and dying evening,
that even then there will still be one more sound:
that of his puny inexhaustible voice, still talking.
I refuse to accept this. I believe that man will not
merely endure: he will prevail. He is immortal, not
because he alone among creatures has an
inexhaustible voice, but because he has a soul, a spirit
capable of compassion and sacrifice and endurance.
The poet's, the writer's, duty is to write about these
things. It is his privilege to help man endure by lifting
his heart, by reminding him of the courage and honor
and hope and pride and compassion and pity and
sacrifice which have been the glory of his past. The
poet's voice need not merely be the record of man,
it can be one of the props, the pillars to help him
endure and prevail.

—William Faulkner, from his Nobel Prize
acceptance speech

Wedding group, White Sulphur Springs,
West Virginia, circa 1900

Wedding

…and wedding party and guests gathered
in the parlor for the bride to cut the cake. I
was caught up too, and the champagne
gave me no pain. The knife was on the
cake, and the cake in tiers was on the
marble top, and Joe's hand on Julia's, the
last symbolic act before the act, Joe in
tight pants and cutaway coat and white
waistcoat of brocaded satin, leaning over
her, his face transformed—he seemed
now the youth which even as a youth he
never showed—he scarcely touched her,
seeming a hovering strength, and I
thought, He is equal to all we've put on
him. Dickie has handled this with skill and
I caught his eye and nodded, Well done;
Dickie in plain view with Amelie beside
him. They were holding hands, their
bodies touching, with the crowd to blame
if any noticed. A handsome woman, raw-
boned but not thin, with lips too full for
her mouth, her eyes all liquid as if the
slightest jar would make them spill. Freshly
widowed, just out of her weeds and with
property. As the knife cut down, I saw her
hand squeeze his. Their eyes met, and she
gave a little toss of her head, and he
followed the flow of her neck.

   …the champagne passed, sparkling in
the thin-stemmed glasses, the silver trays
glowing white and gold, and Aunt Emm
moving among guests and servants like a
fretted ghost, directing here, correcting
there, the servants stiffening at her
approach. She wonders if the food will
hold out; her eye counts the silver; she
passes from kitchen to parlor, mumbling,
"Will it never end?"

—Andrew Lytle, from *The Velvet Horn*

World première, *Gone With The Wind*,
Atlanta, Georgia, 1939

"It was nothing local about it."

"I was in that preemy they had in Atlanta," he would tell visitors sitting on his front porch. "Surrounded by beautiful guls. It wasn't a thing local about it. It was nothing local about it. Listen here. It was a nashnul event and they had me in it—up onto the stage. There was no bobtails at it. Every person at it had paid ten dollars to get in and had to wear his tuxseeder. I was in this uniform. A beautiful gul presented me with it that afternoon in a hotel room...."

"This was a Hollywood, California, gul," he'd continue. "She was from Hollywood, California, and didn't have any part in the pitcher. Out there they have so many beautiful guls that they don't need that they call them a extra and they don't use them for nothing but presenting people with things and having their pitchers taken. They took my pitcher with her. No, it was two of them. One on either side and me in the middle with my arms around each of them's waist and their waist ain't any bigger than a half a dollar...."

"They gimme this uniform and they gimme this soward and they say, 'Now General, we don't want you to start a war on us. All we want you to do is march right up on that stage when you're innerduced tonight and answer a few questions. Think you can do that?' 'Think I can do it!' I say. 'Listen here. I was doing things before you were born,' and they hollered."

...A real limousine came at ten minutes to eight and took them to the theater. It drew up under the marquee at exactly the right time, after the big stars and the director and the author and the governor and the mayor and some less important stars. The police kept traffic from jamming and there were ropes to keep the people off who couldn't go. All the people who couldn't go watched them step out of the limousine into the lights. Then they walked down the red and gold foyer and an usherette in a Confederate cap and little short skirt conducted them to their special seats. The audience was already there and a group of UDC members began to clap when they saw the General in his uniform and that started everybody to clap....

The old man walked up the aisle slowly with his fierce white head high and his hat held over his heart. The orchestra began to play the Confederate Battle Hymm very softly and the UDC members rose as a group and did not sit down again until the General was on the stage. When he reached the center of the stage with Sally Poker just behind him guiding his elbow, the orchestra burst out in a loud rendition of the Battle Hymn and the old man, with real stage presence, gave a vigorous trembling salute and stood at attention until the last blast had died away....

The General stood in the exact center of the spotlight...."Tell me, General," he asked, "how old are you?"

"Niiiiiinnttty-two!" the General screamed.

The young man looked as if this were just about the most impressive thing that had been said all evening. "Ladies and gentlemen," he said, "let's give the General the biggest hand we've got!" and there was applause immediately.

—Flannery O'Connor, from "A Late Encounter with the Enemy" in *A Good Man is Hard to Find*

Cotulla
Faculty
1958

Lyndon Johnson and other elementary school teachers, Cotulla, Texas, 1928

This Was My Rich Inheritance

My granddaddy would ask me questions. He would say, "How many ponies do you have? How many chickens do you have? How many cows are down there at your little place? Tell me about the state of your crops; when are you going to start picking your cotton?"

I would stand there and wiggle my toes in the sand with my finger in my mouth. And if I knew the answers and answered all of his questions correctly, Grandpa would take me in and open a black mahogany desk he had and reach in and get an apple. And I would walk satisfied, and quite proudly, back across the fields along the banks of the river. If I failed, the walk seemed endless—if I hadn't known the answers.

And those hills, and those fields, and the river were the only world that I really had in those years. So I did not know how much more beautiful it was than that of many other boys, for I could imagine nothing else from sky to sky. Yet the sight and the feel of that country somehow or other burned itself into my mind.

We were not a wealthy family, but this was my rich inheritance. All my life I have drawn strength, and something more, from those Texas hills. Sometimes, in the highest councils of the Nation, in this house, I sit back and I can almost feel that rough, unyielding, stocky clay soil between my toes, and it stirs memories that often give me comfort and sometimes give me a pretty firm purpose.

But not all the boys in America had the privilege to grow up in a wide and open country. We can give them something, and we are going to. We can let each of them feel a little of what the first settlers must have felt, as they stood there before the majesty of our great land.

—Lyndon Baines Johnson,
from *The Tragedy of Lyndon Johnson*
by Eric F. Goldman

Fiddler, Reuben, Arkansas, 1968

Cumberland Gap

Me an' my wife an' my wife's pap,
We all live down in Cumberland Gap.
CHORUS
Cumberland Gap, Cumberland Gap,
Mmm*…'way down yonder in Cumberland Gap.

Cumberland Gap is a noted place,
Three kinds of water to wash your face.
CHORUS

The first white man in Cumberland Gap
Was Doctor Walker, an English chap.
CHORUS

Daniel Boone on Pinnacle Rock,
He killed Injuns with his old flintlock.
CHORUS

Lay down, boys, and take a little nap,
Fo'teen miles to the Cumberland Gap.
CHORUS

Old Aunt Dinah, if you don't keer,
Leave my little jug a-settin' right hyer.
CHORUS

Old Aunt Dinah tuck a little spell,
Broke my little jug all to hell.
CHORUS

I've got a woman in Cumberland Gap,
She's got a boy that calls me 'pap.'
CHORUS

Me an' my wife an my wife's pap,
All raise hell in Cumberland Gap.
CHORUS

*A hum that turns into a yell.

—American Folk Song

General store, Moundville, Alabama, 1936

The Store

Until I was thirteen and left Arkansas for good, the Store
was my favorite place to be. Alone and empty in the
mornings, it looked like an unopened present from a
stranger. Opening the front doors was pulling the ribbon
off the unexpected gift. The light would come in softly
(we faced north), easing itself over the shelves of
mackerel, salmon, tobacco, thread. It fell flat on the big
vat of lard and by noontime during the summer the grease
had softened to a thick soup. Whenever I walked into the
Store in the afternoon, I sensed that it was tired. I alone
could hear the slow pulse of its job half done. But just
before bedtime, after numerous people had walked in and
out, had argued over their bills, or joked about their
neighbors, or just dropped in "to give Sister Henderson a
'Hi y'all,'" the promise of magic mornings returned to the
Store and spread itself over the family in washed
life waves.

—Maya Angelou, from *I Know Why The Caged Bird Sings*

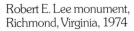
Robert E. Lee monument,
Richmond, Virginia, 1974

Who else could have?

Who else could have made them fight: could have
struck them so aghast with fear and dread as to turn
shoulder to shoulder and face one way and even
stop talking for a while and even after two years of it
keep them still so wrung with terror that some among
them would seriously propose moving their very
capital into a foreign country lest it be ravaged and
pillaged by a people whose entire white male
population would have little more than filled any
one of their larger cities: except Jackson in the Valley
and three separate armies trying to catch him and
none of them ever knowing whether they were just
retreating from a battle or just running into one and
Stuart riding his whole command entirely around
the biggest single armed force this continent ever
saw in order to see what it looked like from behind
and Morgan leading a cavalry charge against a
stranded man-of-war. Who else could have declared
a war against a power with ten times the area and a
hundred times the men and a thousand times the
resources, except men who could believe that all
necessary to conduct a successful war was not
acumen nor shrewdness nor politics nor diplomacy
nor money nor even integrity and simple arithmetic
but just love of land and courage—

—William Faulkner, from "The Bear"
in *The Faulkner Reader*

Tallulah Bankhead with her father and stepmother,
place and date unknown

Tallulah to a Reporter:

"Be careful how you quote me.
No swearing, no naughty cracks.
This is a campaign year, you know,
and I must be discreet.
If I'm not, I'll have the whole
goddam Bankhead family
on my neck."

—Maurice Zolotow,
from *No People Like Show People*

Cowboys on trail in the Southwest, 1967

The Chosen of the Earth

Cowboys could perform terrible labors and
endure bone-grinding hardships and yet
consider themselves the chosen of the
earth; and the grace that redeemed it all in
their own estimation was the fact that they
had gone a-horseback. They were riders,
first and last. I have known cowboys broken
in body and twisted in spirit, bruised by
debt, failure, loneliness, disease and most of
the other afflictions of man, but I have
seldom known one who did not consider
himself phenomenally blessed to have been
a cowboy, or one who could not cancel half
the miseries of existence by dwelling on the
horses he had ridden, the comrades he had
ridden them with, and the manly times he
had had. If the cowboy is a tragic figure, he
is certainly one who will not accept the
tragic view. Instead, he helps his delineators
wring pathos out of tragedy by ameliorating
his own loss into the heroic myth of the
horseman.

—Larry McMurtry,
from "Take My Saddle from the Wall,"
an essay in *In A Narrow Grave*

River baptism near Richmond, Virginia, 1896

Baptism

We drive this Sunday south into the country,
Where a white frame Gothic church stands at the levee.
The Negroes, dressed in black, glistening with the heat,
Come early, carrying lunches, and stay late
In the steaming little church where they sing together.

Across the levee at the old landing they still
Hold their baptisms. A live religion deals
In living symbols; so they prefer the river,
Their untamed font of darkness. I recall one evening
When the red sun broke through colonnades of cloud,

And the two tides met, brown and golden, of earth and air—
Light calm and pure, and that violence of water—
How they went down in white and moaning lamentation,
To the mud-brown flood and under, then broke up singing,
Rolled on the earth, reborn out of death and nature.

Here at the Christian crossroad we note the cleavage
Between the enlightened few with their stoic wisdom,
And the hungry soul of the many whose new Mystery
Is the beat of this spiritual jazz, the loved return
Down to the brown river and wounded Thammuz' blood.

Through all the aseptic channels of the modern
This wild release is pouring; are we who listen,
As the brooding ground and single imploration
Breaks in waves of answer, group-homing passion,
We whites, who can only listen, are blurred with our tears.

—Charles G. Bell, from *Delta Return*

Country road, eastern Kentucky, 1973

Dirt Roads

As you drive south from Louisville you wind through the beautiful Bluegrass country. It is rolling to level. And then in Marion County you come into that narrow ten-mile strip known as the Knobs. This is a band of sharp, conical hills which surround the Bluegrass. You climb steeply out of them up the main escarpment, Muldraugh's Hill, and you are then on what is geologically known as the Pennyroyal plains. There is nothing plainlike about this section, except that it is higher than the country through which you have come. Our hills begin now. And they grow progressively rougher and more rugged the farther south you go. They are tumbled closely together, with deep, steep hollows gashing their sides, and the roads must wind around and between them. Only little dirt roads like ours venture off down the spiny backs of the ridges. Every spur, every hollow, every ridge has its name, but combined they form the Tennessee Ridge, which is like long vertebrae snaking slowly southward into Tennessee. Giles Ridge, then, is like one little bone in the spinal column, and a very small one at that.

I don't know how to tell you of its indescribable beauty. You are in the midst of hills in every direction. There seems no end to them. And as you drive slowly down the road there are openings in the trees through which you look off over sweet, swelling valleys. The Green River valley is to one side of our ridge and the Crooked Creek valley to the other. And there is one place where the road is merely a saddle across the narrow hump of the ridge so that you look down in either direction onto farms and homes and the green fringe of trees down the watercourses. On a clear winter day, when the trees are stripped bare of leaves, I can climb the slope back of our house and look out across five ridges, each rising a little higher than the one before, and I can see the sun glinting on the tin roof of a barn over on the last ridge. In between, the mists will be rising, like pale smoke, hugging close to the streams down in the hollows.

—Janice Holt Giles, from *40 Acres and No Mule*

Riding the Rim of the Bowl

And all the while Detroit kept edging the speeds up, from 150 m.p.h. in 1960 to 155 to 165 to 175 to 180 flat out on the longest straightaway, and the good old boys of Southern stock-car racing stuck right with it. Any speed Detroit would give them they would take right with them into the curve, hard charging even though they began to feel strange things such as the rubber starting to pull right off the tire casing. And God! Good old boys from all over the South roared together after the Stanchion-Speed! Guts!—pouring into Birmingham, Daytona Beach, Randleman, North Carolina; Spartanburg, South Carolina; Weaverville, Hillsboro, North Carolina; Atlanta, Hickory, Bristol, Tennessee; Augusta, Georgia; Richmond, Virginia....

And all the while, standing by in full Shy, in Alumicron suits—there is Detroit hardly able to believe itself, what it has discovered, a breed of good old boys from the fastnesses of the Appalachian hill and flats—a handful from this rare breed—who has given Detroit...speed... and the industry can present it to a whole generation as ...yours. And the Detroit PR men themselves come to the tracks like folk worshippers and the millions go giddy with the thrill of speed. Only Junior Johnson goes about it as if it were...the usual. Junior goes on down to Atlanta for the Dixie 400 and drops by the Federal penitentiary to see his daddy. His daddy is in on his fifth illegal-distillery conviction; in the whiskey business that's just part of it; an able craftsman, an able businessman and the law kept hounding him, that was all. So Junior drops by and then goes on out to the track and gets in his new Ford and sets the qualifying speed record for the Atlanta Dixie 400, 146.301 m.p.h.; later on he tools on back up the road to Ingle Hollow to tend to the automatic chicken houses and the road-grading operation. Yes.

Yet how can you tell that to...anybody...out of the bottom of that bowl as the motor thunder begins to lift up through him like a sigh and his eyeballs glaze over and his hands reach up and there, riding the rim of the bowl, soaring over the ridges, is Junior's yellow Ford...which is his white Chevrolet...which is a White Ghost, forever rousing the good old boys...hard-charging!...up with the automobile into their America, and the hell with arteriosclerotic old boys tugging to hold onto the whole pot with arms of cotton seersucker. Junior!

—Tom Wolfe, from "The Last American Hero"
in *The Kandy-Kolored Tangerine-Flake Streamline Baby*

Start of Daytona 400,
Daytona Beach, Florida, 1974

The Outer Banks,
Avon, North Carolina, 1975

The New Sun Coming Up

Then you know, something as I sat there—
something about the dawn made me think of
America and how the light would come up
slowly over the eastern coast, miles and miles
of it, the Atlantic, and the inlets and bays and
slow tideland rivers with houses on the shore,
all shuttered and sleeping, and this stealthy
light coming up over it all, the fish stakes at
low tide and the ducks winging through the
dawn and a kind of apple-green glow over the
swamplands and the white beaches and the
bays....And I kept thinking of the new sun
coming up over the coast of Virginia and the
Carolinas, and how it must have looked from
those galleons, centuries ago, when after black
night, dawn broke like a trumpet blast, and
there it was, immense and green and glistening
against the crashing seas. And suddenly I
wanted more than anything in my life to go
back there. And I knew I *would* go....

—William Styron, from *Set This House on Fire*

Jonah and the Evolutionists

Darrow: Now, you say, the big fish swallowed Jonah, and he there remained how long? three days? and then he spewed him upon the land. You believe that the big fish was made to swallow Jonah?

Bryan: I am not prepared to say that; the Bible merely says it was done.

Darrow: You don't know whether it was the ordinary run of fish, or made for that purpose?

Bryan: You may guess; you evolutionists guess.

Darrow: But when we do guess, we have a sense to guess right.

Bryan: But do not do it often.

Darrow: You are not prepared to say whether that fish was made especially to swallow a man or not?

Bryan: The Bible doesn't say, so I am not prepared to say.

Darrow: You don't know whether that was fixed up specially for the purpose?

Bryan: No, the Bible doesn't say.

Darrow: But you do believe He made them—that He made such a fish and that it was big enough to swallow Jonah?

Bryan: Yes, sir. Let me add: one miracle is just as easy to believe as another.

Darrow: It is for me.

Bryan: It is for me.

Darrow: Just as hard?

Bryan: It is hard to believe for you, but easy for me. A miracle is a thing performed beyond what man can perform. When you get beyond what man can do, you get within the realm of miracles; and it is just as easy to believe the miracle of Jonah as any other miracle in the Bible.

Darrow: Perfectly easy to believe that Jonah swallowed the whale?

Bryan: If the Bible said so; the Bible doesn't make as extreme statements as evolutionists do.

—from *The State of Tennessee* v. *John Thomas Scopes*

Coon dogs, Renfroe Valley, Kentucky, 1975

Not Many Coons Like That One

The hounds had treed him first at midnight; now at half past two they had him again. It was the same coon, the big one: there was no mistaking the frantic yapping of the hounds.

Theron and his father and Verne Luttrell, his tenant, stopped, panting, and turned upon each other's faces the cold, intense white light, like distilled moonlight, of the carbide lamps, giant cyclops eyes gleaming out of the forehead of each. The light drained the faces of all color and all but the shallowest depth. They stood listening for a moment, then agreed without words which direction the sound was from and set off at a lope through the trees that danced in the bobbing lights.

This coon had made fools of them, dogs as well as men, from early evening, had led them cursing through swamps and canebrakes, then backtracked and led them through the same ones again, had crossed water so many times that the hounds were in a frenzy of confusion, then got so far ahead of them that he doubled and crossed his own scent, and would have been in the next county before the dogs came out of their maze had the wind not taken a shift.

Now, as they tore through a gulley and scrambled up the bank, the barking grew louder and more excited, and when they started across the moonlit clearing to the woods Verne Luttrell commenced calling, "Hold im, Prince. Hold im, Queen. Hold im, Champ." And the hounds reached such a pitch that their barks became whines of helpless excitement....

The dogs were old, well-trained, and knew the sound of the final axe stroke on a hollow tree. They watched, almost silent now in strained expectancy, and those in the way of the fall moved aside exactly enough while the others closed ranks and narrowed their ring as Verne Luttrell stepped back.

The tree fell with a dry, splintery crash. There was a spray of dirt exploded from the ground, the rip and crack of dead branches shattering, a howl from the dogs. Then, in a sudden hush, a readjustment of carbide lamps revealed nine eager but wary hounds and an unperturbed, ready, fat old coon who stood on his hind legs slowly circling, his front paws cocked like a boxer's, revolving on his tail inside the flexible, undulating, spotted dog-ring which surged cautiously in as his back was turned and bulged swiftly out again as his front came round.

"Git im, dawg!" said Verne Luttrell.

The one called Queen, acknowledged the leader, went in to the chorus of the others. There was a blur of spots and stripes, a sudden puff of fur loosened upon the air, a yelp, and Queen, with one long ear slit through and streaming blood, howled ignominiously out of the ring.

At the smell of blood the pack closed in. It became a snarling, yelping, spotted pinwheel, swelling and contracting, until suddenly it slowed, came into focus, and there in the center of things, in the circle of light, lay the one called Champ, his throat slit wide, kicking feebly while the last of his dark blood flowed upon the ground. Meanwhile the coon, with no more thought of him, had resumed that slow circle, only spiraling slightly now to move the ring away from this obstacle to his defence....

"Let im go?" said Verne. "Let im go! Hell, he don't want to go nowhere. Let im go! That was my hound he killed, not one of yourn. And he was my best one, too."

"Well, I'll give you one of mine. For a wedding present," said the Captain.

And even in that cold light, Theron saw, or rather remembered later, that Verne Luttrell colored at this allusion to his marriage. "I don't want one of yourn. Which one?"

"Whichever you say," said the Captain. "But let the coon go. He has outsmarted us all night and he has outfought us. Call off the dogs—or rather, beat them off—while we still have some of them left. I got lots of dogs, but not many coons like that to run them on."

—William Humphrey, from *Home from the Hill*

Cotton day, Eutaw, Alabama, 1893

The Greatest Crop Heaven Ever Gave

Thirty years ago our Great-Aunt Narcissa began telling us the cotton kingdom was doomed—the world market was slipping irrevocably from us, we should begin substituting other crops. For at least fifteen years all of us have been fully aware that our reckoning day for cotton would inevitably come to hand, but even under these circumstances we have not turned away from cotton. We have gone right on plowing and planting. It is never easy for a people to give up a hundred-year-old tradition —our lives and our fathers' fathers' lives have been built around cotton. We have bought our clothes with a bale of cotton; we have built our houses with cotton money; we have sold a bale of cotton to pay our way through school. We have even campaigned in politics atop a cotton bale. And even our Great-Aunt Narcissa stated once in public that she did not care what anybody in Washington or anywhere else in the world said about cotton, it still was the greatest crop that heaven ever gave to any country.

—Ben Robertson, from *Red Hills and Cotton*

Oklahoma cheerleaders,
Texas-Oklahoma football game, Dallas, Texas, 1958

The Best Group He'll Ever Be With

…there is no sin in not liking to play, …it's a
mistake for a boy to be there if he doesn't want to.
But if he loves it it's an opportunity to make himself a
part of a big thing. To be associated with the best
group of kids in the world.

It doesn't have to be at Alabama. If the system is
right, no matter where he plays he's with the best
group he'll ever be with. His teammates.

He has been accepted by an institution and has
been given an alma mater, something to tie to. He is
going to go a lot of places, firstclass, and perform
before thousands of people, even millions, including
his family and people he loves.

He'll be getting his foot in the door for the future,
gaining recognition, learning lessons about living.
There will be times when he'll hate that smelly
uniform, and times when he gets mad at his best
friend, and times when he's cussing his coach under
his breath. He's going to have to work hard.

But when it comes down to those Saturdays, and
the band's playing and the cold shivers are running
down his back, he'll *know* how much it means to
him. If he loves it, and gives it everything he has, he's
one of the luckiest young men in the world.

—Paul W. Bryant and John Underwood,
from *Bear, The Hard Life and Good Times
of Alabama's Coach Bryant*

So Get a Few Laughs
and Do the Best You Can

We are just here for a spell and pass on. Any man that thinks civilization has advanced is an egotist.…We know a lot of things we used to dident know, but we dont know any way to prevent 'em happening.

We have more tooth paste on the market and more misery in our courts than at any time in our existence. There aint nothing to life but satisfaction.

Indians and primitive races were the highest civilized because they were more satisfied and they depended less on each other and took less from each other. We couldent live a day without depending on everybody. So our civilization has given us no liberty or independence.

So get a few laughs and do the best you can. Take nothing serious for nothing is certainly depending on this generation. Each one lives in spite of the previous one and not because of it.

And dont have an ideal to work for. That's like riding towards a mirage of a lake. When you get there, it aint there. Believe in something for another world, but dont be too set on what it is, and then you wont start out that life with a disappointment. Live your life so that whenever you lose you are ahead.

—Will Rogers, from *The Will Rogers Book*
by Paula McSpadden Love

Chrétien Point Plantation, Sunset,
Louisiana, 1946

Brave Glitter Against a Black Night

Because now people—fathers and mothers and sisters and kin
and sweethearts of those young men—were coming to Oxford
from further away than Jefferson—families with food and
bedding and servants, to bivouac among the families, the houses,
of Oxford itself, to watch the gallant mimic marching and
counter-marching of the sons and the brothers, drawn all of
them, rich and poor, aristocrat and redneck, by what is probably
the most moving mass-sight of all human mass-experience, far
more so than the spectacle of so many virgins going to be
sacrificed to some heathen Principle, some Priapus—the sight
of young men, the light quick bones, the bright gallant deluded
blood and flesh dressed in a martial glitter of brass and plumes,
marching away to a battle. And there would be music at night—
fiddle and triangle among the blazing candles, the blowing of
curtains in tall windows on the April darkness, the swing of
crinoline indiscriminate within the circle of plain gray cuff of the
soldier or the banded gold of rank, of any army even if not a war
of gentlemen, where private and colonel called each other by
their given names not as one farmer to another across a halted
plow in a field or across a counter in a store laden with calico and
cheese and strap oil, but as one man to another above the suave
powdered shoulders of women, above the two raised glasses of
scuppernong claret or bought champagne—music, the nightly
repetitive last waltz as the days passed and the company waited
to move, the brave trivial glitter against a black night not
catastrophic but merely background, the perennial last scented
spring of youth....

—William Faulkner, from *Absalom! Absalom!*

The Law Is a Dangerous Thing

"Does Press Tussie live here?" the stranger asked.

"Yep, he does," Grandpa said. "I'm Press Tussie."

"I'm Eddie McConnell," the stranger said, a-shakin Grandpa's hand. "I'm the county attendance officer."

"What's that?" Grandpa asked. "Is it one of them A.B.C. letter offices?"

"No, it's not that kind of an office," Eddie McConnell said. "I'm to see that children in this county go to school. It's been reported to me that you have a boy here of school age that is not enrolled in this county and has never gone to school a day in his life."

"Who reported that?" Grandpa asked.

"I'm not to tell you that, Mr. Tussie," Eddie McConnell said. "I just want to know if this is a fact. How old is your boy?"

"Don't know exactly," Grandpa said. "'Spect he's in the neighborhood of thirteen, fourteen, maybe fifteen."

"And he's never gone to school a day in his life?"

"Nope."

"Is this the boy?" he asked Grandpa, pointin to me.

"Yep, that's Sid."

"Now, Mr. Tussie, it's not for the want of clothes you haven't sent him, is it?" Eddie McConnell asked. "He's wearin good clothes and good shoes."

"Nope, it's not that," Grandpa said. "I never went to school a day in my life and I'm still a-livin. I've reached my three score year and ten."

"But there's a law in Kentucky that now compels you to send your children to school," Eddie McConnell said. "If you don't send your children to school you can be brought before the county judge and fined!"

"A law," Grandpa said. "Shucks, I didn't know that."

"You'll find out about this law if you don't have this boy in school by Monday," Eddie McConnell told Grandpa.

"I'll have 'im there before Monday if that's the law," Grandpa said. "I'll have 'im there day after tomorrow."

"He's in the Six Hickories School," Eddie McConnell said. "Do you know where that schoolhouse is?"

"Yep—yep, I do," Grandpa said with a tremblin voice.

I heard Grandma cough at the kitchen winder. I thought I heard Aunt Vittie laugh.

"Do you know where it is, young man?" he asked me.

"Yes, I know where it's at," I said.

"Then this will be all," Eddie McConnell said. "I'll expect 'im in school by Monday. If he's not there, you can see the county judge."

"He'll be there," Grandpa said.

"Good day, Mr. Tussie," Mr. McConnell said as he turned to go away.

"Ssslon-long," Grandpa said with a weak tremblin voice.

"Gee, Grandpa," I said, "I hate to go to school. I can't bear to go back to that schoolhouse again."

"But you'll haf to go, Sid," Grandpa said. "It's the law. I didn't know it was the law. I didn't know the law could make you send a boy to school. Things have changed since I was a boy."

"Somebody's a-doin a lot of reportin," Grandma said, stickin her head outten the kitchen winder. "I think it's some of your kinfolks, Press."

"The Law is a dangerous thing," Grandpa said.

—Jesse Stuart, from *Taps for Private Tussie*

Wagon wheels, Madison, Georgia, 1974

The Road Is Never the Dreamed One

Time and chance happened to them—in America as in Ecclesiastes. They were called to Texas, to California—and the first were last, and the last first, and many were called but few chosen. I was Southern, I was old.

Like other Southerners I have known from the start that the way is long, and that we live and leave what record we can of our hopes, of the cry in our hearts. We plow the water, and it is the spirit alone that is ever free, and it is only memory that has no time. How often do we picture the way ahead and dream of it and plan? But the actual road is never the dreamed one, and the sights that we start out to see are not the scenes that we remember. It is not the cathedral that lives. It is something else, the sudden and the unexpected. Not the great famed thing, but a mist, an expression on a face, a whisper. Often it is the fragile things of a moment that never die, that one remembers on and on through a life. The lines of a mountain lie in the mind, a sunset never fades, a peach blossom never shatters. The light of a star shines on, and there is the dim glimmer of distant lightning, and the good that one has done and the evil. It is regret that never dies.

Like other Southerners, I have known from the start that there would be no new Texas for us, no California. I have always known that the procession we march in has already arrived in the promised land. It is here for us, not there. In the South, I have known that from our time on, we would be obliged to find what it is we look for within ourselves. It is not to be found in change of scene, nor in pulling up stakes. It is ourselves now that we must settle, it is the state that we must take hold of, we must enrich old fields and stop erosion. It is in the state that we can find the riches, the perfect security, and the peace. We cannot turn our backs—we cannot pick up and leave any longer. We are old and we must do what all who are old must do; there is the responsibility to assume and the duty. No one can be young always. Who would wish to be? Texas is Carolina now, and California is Texas, and we can fly to them all in a night.

—Ben Robertson, from *Red Hills and Cotton*

Ty Cobb stealing third base,
place and date unknown

A Long Journey Done

Royston, Ga., July 20, 1961

It was a hot afternoon when they came to the small white chapel
on the hill in Cornelia, where soft breezes from the blue mountains
beyond brushed across the apple trees and through the open
windows. Thunderheads gathered behind the hills, briefly making
their threat of a summer storm and then surrendering again before
the fire of a July sun. Stillness fell on the hill in Cornelia, and they
began their farewell to Tyrus Raymond Cobb.

They came from Detroit and California, from Royston and from
down the street, those who were close and devoted to the greatest
baseball player who ever lived. Mickey Cochrane, Ray Schalk,
and Nap Rucker were there, men of his own breed and time who knew
him on other hot afternoons. And friends made in later years as
the flame flickered and this day drew nearer.

Outside, small boys in dungarees gathered along the sidewalk
and old men in overalls stood under the trees and their faces
reflected the presence of immortality. The gentle strains of "Rock
of Ages" filled the little chapel and floated softly through the
windows as they have for a hundred years and more in these firm
clay hills. The preacher said he wasn't preaching Ty Cobb's
funeral, for as you and I and all the rest will do, Ty Cobb preached his
own. He did say, as a close friend and minister, that in those last
months and days Ty Cobb had faced his Maker squarely, as good
men do.

And then, the last journey. Down the hill past husky policemen
standing straight with hats held over their hearts in silent salute.
Past service stations and stores where patrons and proprietors
paused to watch, brushed briefly by history. Out of the hills and
into the valleys, where mountain folk stopped their work in cotton
fields to lean on hoe handles and say their own farewell. Old
women in cloth bonnets, and old men in straw hats toiled on land
little changed from the time Cobb left it many years ago.

Through Carnesville and on toward Royston, and then past
Cobb Memorial Hospital where patients and nurses lined the
windows and the steps, and remembered their debt to the man who
held this place so close to his heart. The procession went into
Royston, and past the service station where once stood the house
Cobb lived in before baseball called him to Augusta, and to
Detroit, and to immortality.

—Jim Minter, from *The Atlanta Journal*

Deer, Everglades Park, Florida, 1971

Sanctuary

You must remember this when I am gone,
And tell your sons—for you will have tall sons,
And times will come when answers will not wait.
Remember this: if ever defeat is black
Upon your eyelids, go to the wilderness
In the dread last of trouble, for your foe
Tangles there, more than you, and paths are strange
To him, that are your paths, in the wilderness,
And were your fathers' paths, and once were mine.

You must remember this, and mark it well
As I have told it—what my eyes have seen
And where my feet have walked beyond forgetting.
But tell it not often, tell it only at last
When your sons know what blood runs in their veins.
And when the danger comes, as come it will,
Go as your fathers went with woodsman's eyes
Uncursed, unflinching, studying only the path.

First, what you cannot carry, burn or hide.
Leave nothing here for *him* to take or eat.
Bury, perhaps, what you can surely find
If good chance ever bring you back again.
Level the crops. Take only what you need:
A little corn for an ash-cake, a little
Side-meat for your three days' wilderness ride.
Horses for your women and your children,
And one to lead, if you should have that many.
Then go. At once. Do not wait until
You see *his* great dust rising in the valley.
Then it will be too late.
Go when you hear that he has crossed Will's Ford.
Others will know and pass the word to you—
A tap on the blinds, a hoot-owl's cry at dusk.

Do not look back. You can see your roof afire
When you reach high ground. Yet do not look.
Do not turn. Do not look back.
Go further on. Go high. Go deep.

The line of this rail-fence east across the old-fields
Leads to the cane-bottoms. Back of that,
A white-oak tree beside a spring, the one
Chopped with three blazes on the hillward side.

There pick up the trail. I think it was
A buffalo path once or an Indian road.
You follow it three days along the ridge
Until you reach the spruce woods. Then a cliff
Breaks, where the trees are thickest, and you look
Into a cove, and right across, Chilhowee
Is suddenly there, and you are home at last.
Sweet springs of mountain water in that cove
Run always. Deer and wild turkey range.
Your kin, knowing the way, long there before you
Will have good fires and kettles on to boil,
Bough-shelters reared and thick beds of balsam.
There in tall timber you will be as free
As were your fathers once when Tryon raged
In Carolina hunting Regulators,
Or Tarleton rode to hang the old-time Whigs.
Some tell how in that valley young Sam Houston
Lived long ago with his brother, Oo-loo-te-ka,
Reading Homer among the Cherokee;
And others say a Spaniard may have found it
Far from De Soto's wandering turned aside,
And left his legend on a boulder there.
And some that this was a sacred place to all
Old Indian tribes before the Cherokee
Came to our eastern mountains. Men have found
Images carved in bird-shapes there and faces
Moulded into the great kind look of gods.
These old tales are like prayers. I only know
This is the secret refuge of our race
Told only from a father to his son,
A trust laid on your lips, as though a vow
To generations past and yet to come.
There, from the bluffs above, you may at last
Look back to all you left, and trace
His dust and flame, and plan your harrying
If you would gnaw his ravaging flank, or smite
Him in his glut among the smouldering ricks.
Or else, forgetting ruin, you may lie
On sweet grass by a mountain stream, to watch
The last wild eagle soar or the last raven
Cherish his brood within their rocky nest,
Or see, when mountain shadows first grow long,
The last enchanted white deer come to drink.

—Donald Davidson, from *Lee in the Mountains and Other Poems*

Tenant farmers, Eutaw, Alabama, 1937

Go Down, Death

"And God said: Go down,
    Death, go down,
Go down to Savannah,
    Georgia,
Down in Yamacraw,
And find Sister Caroline.
She's borne the burden
    and heat of the day,
She's labored long in
    my vineyard,
And she's tired—
She's weary—
Go down, Death,
    and bring her to me...."

—James Weldon Johnson,
    from *God's Trombones*

Dry Run Christian Church,
Shenandoah Valley, Virginia, 1973

When Jericho Rises

And everywhere the land is part of the mind. There is
indeed this mystery. And when Jericho rises, bearing
with it people and customs, it rises upon the land. But
how to comprehend it? We can go anywhere, but what
is the final meaning? Some of it is in detail, but maybe
the whole of Jericho is in the sum of them? But what
details are the right ones? In the air without a body, we
are all poets. Afternoon light lies on cotton, but it flashes
on a church. That is something we Spirits must do: we
must flash on a church.

It is clean here, and empty. But no one would come
who did not believe. There is an intensity of gentleness
beyond any description, and in silence a sense of
congregation like layers of souls, close to each other,
caring. We have come. We should have.

—James Dickey, from *Jericho, The South Beheld*

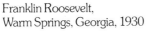
Franklin Roosevelt,
Warm Springs, Georgia, 1930

Visiting with Farmers

He seemed to know dozens of people, politicians and farmers;
moreover, he knew the countryside with an intimacy that must have
been gained by close and repeated investigation....[He] spent part of
nearly every day, sometimes whole days, exploring the back roads,
visiting with farmers—simply driving into yards, pulling up under the
inevitable chinaberry tree, and hailing whomever he could see. In these
casual conversations, he had learned more about farmers' grievances
than he would ever have discovered in New York, where they were
filtered to him through professionals, or could have learned in Hyde
Park on what was not a farm but an estate....There were no barriers,
or anyway none such as existed wherever else he went. He learned
something real about life down the dirt roads and in the farmyards of
Meriwether County, and he learned it for good.

—Rexford G. Tugwell, from *FDR: Architect of An Era*

Rich Days Followed by Empty Ones

Men still set out to find the tiny fish wherever the signs indicate that they may be. They study the water surfaces, they recall their experiences of other years in certain places, they watch for the down-sweeping gulls that may indicate a concentration of the shelled things. As during the earlier years, rich days will be followed by empty ones and men will wait in the bitter glare of the waters.

—Harnett T. Kane, from *Deep Delta Country*

Evergreen Plantation slave cabins,
Mississippi River Road, Louisiana, 1947

Our Particular Cabin

I was born in a typical log cabin, about fourteen by sixteen feet square. In this cabin I lived with my mother and a brother and sister till after the Civil War, when we were all declared free.

The cabin was not only our living-place, but was also used as the kitchen for the plantation. My mother was the plantation cook. The cabin was without glass windows; it had only openings in the side which let in the light, and also the cold, chilly air of winter. There was a door to the cabin—that is, something that was called a door—but the uncertain hinges by which it was hung, and the large cracks in it, to say nothing of the fact that it was too small, made the room a very uncomfortable one. In addition to these openings there was, in the lower right-hand corner of the room, the "cat-hole"—a contrivance which almost every mansion or cabin in Virginia possessed during the antebellum period. The "cat-hole" was a square opening, about seven by eight inches, provided for the purpose of letting the cat pass in and out of the house at will during the night. In the case of our particular cabin I could never understand the necessity for this convenience, since there were at least a half-dozen other places in the cabin that would have accommodated the cats. There was no wooden floor in our cabin, the naked earth being used as a floor. In the centre of the earthen floor there was a large, deep opening covered with boards, which was used as a place in which to store sweet potatoes during the winter. An impression of this potato-hole is very distinctly engraved upon my memory, because I recall that during the process of putting the potatoes in or taking them out I would often come into possession of one or two, which I roasted and thoroughly enjoyed. There was no cooking-stove on our plantation, and all the cooking for the whites and slaves my mother had to do over an open fireplace, mostly in pots and "skillets." While the poorly built log cabin caused us to suffer with cold in the winter, the heat from the open fireplace in summer was equally trying.

—Booker T. Washington, from *Up from Slavery*

Mallards in flight, Atlantic flyway, 1968

What Ducks Require

Ducks require no ship and sail
Bellied on the foamy skies,
Who scud north. Male and female
Make a slight nest to arise
Where they overtake the spring,
Which clogs with muddy going.

The zone unready. But the pond,
Eye of a bleak Cyclops visage, catches
Such glints of hyacinth and bland
As bloom in aquarelles of ditches
On a cold spring ground, a freak,
A weathering chance even in the wrack.

The half-householders for estate
Beam their floor with ribs of grass,
Disdain your mortises and slate
And Lar who invalided lies,
The marsh quakes dangerous, the port
Where wet and dry precisely start.

Furled, then, the quadrate wing
From the lewd eye and fowler's gun
Till in that wet sequestering,
Webtoed, the progeny is done,
Cold-hatched, the infant prodigy tries
To preen his feathers for the skies.

Prodigious in his wide degrees
Who where the winds and waters blow
On raveling banks of fissured seas
In reeds nestles, or will rise and go
Where Capricornus dips his hooves
In the blue chasm of no wharves.

—John Crowe Ransom,
from *Selected Poems*

Coca-Cola truck, Knoxville, Tennessee, 1909

It Is a Fine Thing—Certain....

You know how I suffer with headaches. Well some days ago a
friend suggested that I try Coca-Cola. I did & was relieved. Some
days later I again tried it & was again relieved. I determined to
find out about it—investigation showed that it was owned by
parties unable to put it fairly before the people. I determined to
put money into it & a little influence. I put $500 of the first & am
putting a goodly portion of what I have of the last. Do you know
a dispenser of soda water in Nashville who will take hold of it for
me? I enclose a card. Now to any retailer or soda fountain man
who will allow me to issue one hundred and twenty eight of these
free cards which will require 1 gallon (128 ounces) of Coca-Cola
syrup, I will send gratis 2 gallons of Coca-Cola syrup. Then if he
will send me the names of 128 ladies or gentlemen I will mail
them each a free ticket to his fountain & he will have as
compensation 128 more ounces to sell to those who will certainly
want more. Now I don't want to make a merchant or peddler
out of you but if you could either send me the name of a party
who wants to engage to introduce it into Nashville (the best soda
fountain town South I am told) I will make it interesting to him. I
enclose circulars. It is a fine thing—certain....

—Asa G. Candler, from *Atlanta and Its Environs*
by Franklin M. Garrett

Ku Klux Klan, Mississippi, 1964

Were You There When They Crucified My Lord?

Were you there, when they crucified my Lord?
Were you there, when they crucified my Lord?
Oh, sometimes it causes me to tremble, tremble, tremble.
Were you there, when they crucified my Lord?

Were you there, when they nailed him to the tree?
Were you there, when they nailed him to the tree?
Oh, sometimes it causes me to tremble, tremble, tremble.
Were you there, when they nailed him to the tree?

Were you there, when they pierced him in the side?
Were you there, when they pierced him in the side?
Oh, sometimes it causes me to tremble, tremble, tremble.
Were you there, when they pierced him in the side?

Were you there, when the sun refused to shine?
Were you there, when the sun refused to shine?
Oh, sometimes it causes me to tremble, tremble, tremble.
Were you there, when the sun refused to shine?

Were you there, when they laid him in the tomb?
Were you there, when they laid him in the tomb?
Oh, sometimes it causes me to tremble, tremble, tremble.
Were you there, when they laid him in the tomb?

—Negro Spiritual

The *Mary S. Blees* on the Tombigbee River, Murphy's Bluff, Alabama, date unknown

The Boys' Ambition

When I was a boy, there was but one permanent ambition among my comrades in our village on the west bank of the Mississippi River. That was, to be a steamboatman. We had transient ambitions of other sorts, but they were only transient....

Once a day a cheap, gaudy packet arrived upward from St. Louis, and another downward from Keokuk. Before these events, the day was glorious with expectancy; after them, the day was a dead and empty thing....I can picture that old time to myself now, just as it was then: the white town drowsing in the sunshine of a summer's morning; the streets empty, or pretty nearly so; one or two clerks sitting in front of the Water Street stores...; a sow and a litter of pigs loafing along the sidewalk...; two or three lonely little freight piles scattered about the "levee"; a pile of "skids" on the slope of the stone-paved wharf, and the fragrant town drunkard asleep in the shadow of them; two or three wood flats at the head of the wharf, but nobody to listen to the peaceful lapping of the wavelets against them....

"S-t-e-a-m-boat a-comin'!" and the scene changes! The town drunkard stirs, the clerks wake up, a furious clatter of drays follows, every house and store pours out a human contribution, and all in a twinkling the dead town is alive and moving. Drays, carts, men, boys, all go hurrying from many quarters to a common center, the wharf. Assembled there, the people fasten their eyes upon the coming boat as upon a wonder they are seeing for the first time. And the boat *is* rather a handsome sight, too. She is long and sharp and trim and pretty; she has two tall, fancy-topped chimneys, with a gilded device of some kind swung between them; a fanciful pilothouse, all glass and "gingerbread"...; the paddle-boxes are gorgeous with a picture or with gilded rays above the boat's name; the boiler deck, the hurricane deck, and the texas deck are fenced and ornamented with clean white railings; there is a flag gallantly flying from the jack-staff; the furnace doors are open and the fires glaring bravely; the upper decks are black with passengers; the captain stands by the big bell, calm, imposing, the envy of all; great volumes of the blackest smoke are rolling and tumbling out of the chimneys—a husbanded grandeur created with a bit of pitch pine just before arriving at a town; the crew are grouped on the forecastle; the broad stage is run far out over the port bow, and an envied deck hand stands picturesquely on the end of it with a coil of rope in his hand;...the captain lifts his hand, a bell rings, the wheels stop; then they turn back, churning the water to foam, and the steamer is at rest. Then such a scramble as there is to get aboard, and to get ashore, and to take in freight and to discharge freight, all at one and the same time; and such a yelling and cursing as the mates facilitate it all with! Ten minutes later the steamer is under way again, with no flag on the jack-staff and no black smoke issuing from the chimneys. After ten more minutes the town is dead again, and the town drunkard asleep by the skids once more.

—Mark Twain, from *Life on the Mississippi*

On the First Saturday in May

For now we approach the event about which no one can write quite truthfully. The legends are too strong. A man may go to Miami or Baltimore or Saratoga feeling no particular way and may report what he sees. But the Kentucky Derby must be approached with an attitude. He may go Southern and wave his julep and request the band to play "Dixie." He may denounce the entire enterprise as a scandalous piece of commercialization. He may hail the winner as the culmination of three hundred years of selective

Hundredth running of the Kentucky Derby, Louisville, Kentucky, 1974

breeding or belittle him as a lucky three-year-old forced to run too far too early in the year. He may call the tinsel glittering or call it tawdry.

But some attitude he must take. A man who writes of the Kentucky Derby as he would about the running of the Belmont Stakes would have his license taken up and his social security number cancelled, and nobody would read him, either.

Never having studied astronomy, this department cannot tell you whether the moon is closest to the earth on the first Saturday in May, or Jupiter is in recession, or the yonge sunne hath in the Ram his halfe-course y-runne. But sondry folk longen—now we got Chaucer—to go on pilgrimages, and from all over the racing world a course is laid in Louisville, Ky.

—Joe H. Palmer, from *This Was Racing*

American history class,
Hampton Institute, Hampton, Virginia, 1899

Their Arrows Are Broken

As a race they have withered from the land. Their
arrows are broken, and their springs are dried up: their
cabins are in the dust. Their council has long since gone
out on the shore, and their war-cry is fast dying out to
the untrodden west. Slowly and sadly they climb the
mountains and read their doom in the setting sun.
They are shrinking before the mighty tide which is
pressing them away; they must soon hear the roar of
the last wave, which will settle over them forever. Ages
hence, the inquisitive white man, as he stands by some
growing city, will ponder on the structure of their
disturbed remains and wonder to what manner of
person they belonged. They will live only in the songs
and chronicles of their exterminators. Let these be
faithful to their rude virtues as men, and pay due
tribute to their unhappy fate as a people.

—Sam Houston, from "A Tribute to the Indians,"
a speech in the United States Senate

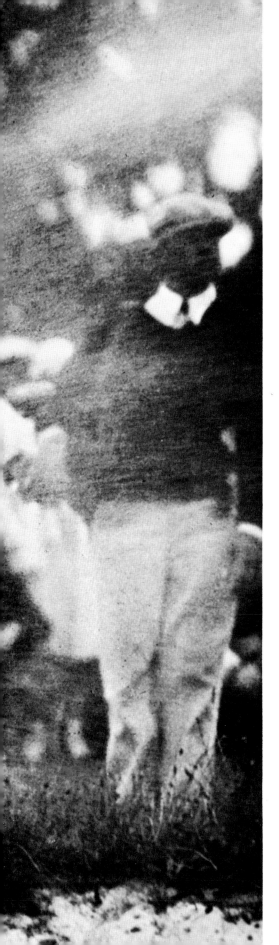

Bobby Jones, Pebble Beach, California, 1929

"Will Ye No' Come Back Again?"

When we welcome back Mr. Jones to St. Andrews, we welcome an old and dearly loved friend—as we welcomed him on his last visit in 1936 when he played around the Old Course attended, one might well imagine, by practically the entire population of the town.

We welcome him for his own sake; we welcome him also as an ambassador in the cause of international understanding and good will which the competition of this week is designed to promote. We welcome him moreover not only as a distinguished golfer but as a man of outstanding character, courage, and accomplishment well worthy to adorn the Roll of our Honorary Burgesses. And that an American should once again be entered in that roll may well be thought timely, for it is just one year short of two hundred years ago, in October 1759, that our predecessors welcomed Dr. Benjamin Franklin of Philadelphia and accorded him the privileges of a Burgess and Guild Brother of the city of St. Andrews.

What these privileges now are in any tangible sense, even the Town Clerk hesitates to suggest—though Mr. Jones may be interested to know that any that are ever mentioned relate specifically to the links—to cart shells, to take divots, and to dry one's washing upon the first and last fairways of the Old Course.

Herb Wind…wrote…"Bobby spoke for ten minutes, beautifully and movingly.…He said near the end of his talk, 'I could take out of my life everything except my experiences at St. Andrews and I'd still have a rich, full life.' He left the stage and got into his electric golf cart. As he directed it down the center aisle to leave, the whole hall spontaneously burst into the old Scottish song 'Will Ye No' Come Back Again?'"

—Provost of St. Andrews, Scotland, and
Herbert Warren Wind, from *Golf Is My Game*
by Robert Tyre Jones, Jr.

Caretaker among Union tombstones,
Andersonville, Georgia, 1970

He Wore Blue, He Wore Butternut

O sad maimed Future! Where is your prime
inventor? The ocean covered him with barnacles
when the *Monitor* went down. Where is the saint
whose scalpel or microscope was intended to
still the scream of cancer? We Federals spattered
his skull at Missionary Ridge. O long discordant
Future drowned in tears, as now my soul is
drowning! Where is the President whose power
and nobility might have led a healed Nation to
world-enfolding glory? The fever took him at
Rock Island, in Arkansas, in Libby Prison, at
Fort Delaware. He wore blue, he wore butternut.
He drew a lanyard, he tore the paper of a
cartridge with his teeth, he galloped behind
John Morgan, he rode to meet the lead on that
last charge of Farnsworth's in a Pennsylvania
glen. Minister and explorer, balloonist and poet,
botanist and judge, geologist and astronomer
and man with songs to sing...they are clavicles
under leaves at Perryville, ribs and phalanges in
the soil of Iuka, they are a bone at Seven Pines, a
bone at Antietam, bones in battles yet to be
sweated, they are in the soil instead of walking,
the moss has them.

—MacKinlay Kantor, from *Andersonville*

Fisherman, Okeefenokee Swamp, Georgia, 1959

Rabbits, Cooking Suppers

It was all swamp, that huge expanse below
and beyond us. The lowest rain clouds
began to dissipate over it and we could
trace the outlines of cypresses and water
tupelos and gums. The dark and grey-greens
of their leaves were merged in the lingering
shadow. Thunder still rolled far away, but
the only rain was a soft dripping from the
oaks and prickly ashes near the porch,
whenever the wind came up to shake the
drops.

Then, from the swamp across the river,
columns of vapor began to rise—a hundred
spirals which looked like the tenuous smoke
of a hundred separate fires. The heat of the
earth rising into the wet air was causing
these columns of smoke, I knew. They
weren't smoke at all, just a form of ground
fog. And yet there was fresh mystery in the
display—the mystery of a swamp scarcely
ever penetrated, still called impenetrable,
beyond the river banks....Near the porch a
feathery Torreya trembled in a brief gust and
shook off a fresh shower of droplets. But I
kept my eyes on the distant columns of
vapor.

"See those?" my friend the woodsman
said. "Look like smoke, but they ain't, of
course. We used to say, though"—he
grinned—"used to say, 'That's rabbits. Rabbits,
cookin' up their suppers.'"

In the Garden of Eden.

—Gloria Jahoda, from *The Other Florida*

Moonshine still, West Virginia, 1934

They Fotch Me!

Judge: Well, sir! I want to know why it is that you, who look like an honest man, persist in pursuing this illicit whiskey business? I want to know whether, after the lenience shown you by this court, you expect to come back here any more.

Defendant: Why, bygosh, jedge. I didn't *come* here *this* time!

Judge: Well, then, how did you get here?

Defendant: They fotch me! Yes, sir, jedge, they fotch me! I didn't *come* here, jedge, and I never will *come* here, you needn't be oneasy about that.

—Joseph Earl Dabney,
from a North Carolina trial,
in *Mountain Spirits*

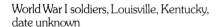
World War I soldiers, Louisville, Kentucky,
date unknown

Tough Jes Like a Hickory Pole

Captain E. C. B. Danforth, Jr., was my
company commander. He come from Augusta,
and was a Georgia "Cracker." He was a
Harvard man. That didn't mean nothing to me
in those days. It didn't mean much to the other
boys either. All we knowed was that like the
Major he had a heap of larnin'. He was tall
and tough jes like a hickory pole. He must
have been about twenty-three or twenty-four
years old, and he had as much sense as a
much older man. He was the fightinest man,
too, and when he was in action our boys used
to say he was that hard that the bullets used
to bounce off'n him. The Major and the
Captain together were as good a combination
as a pair of Red Bones when you have them
out after the foxes. They ran together. If ever
I have to go to war agin I'm a-telling you I
wouldn't ask for anything more than to have
them two leading me. Wherever they go I am
willing to follow. And that's jes about how
most of the other boys under them feel.

My own platoon was made up of a gang of
the toughest and most hard-boiled doughboys
I ever heard tell of. There were bartenders,
saloon bouncers, ice men, coal miners, dirt
farmers, actors, mill hands, and city boys who
had growed up in the back alleys and learned
to scrap ever since they were knee high to a
duck. They were mixed up from 'most every
country. They were as hard as a forest full
of oaks and they were meaner and more full
of fight than a hive of wild bees. They could
out-swear, out-drink, and out-cuss any other
crowd of men I have ever knowed. They sorter
looked upon leave-breaking as a divine right.

—from *Sergeant York, His Own Life Story
and War Diary*

A man and a pig, Tifton, Georgia, 1938

The Friendliness of Pigs

One morning as I passed the pen he grunted—spoke, I may say—
in such a pleasant friendly way that I had to stop and return his
greeting; then, taking an apple from my pocket, I placed it in his
trough....He turned it over with his snout, then looked up and said
something like "thank you" in a series of gentle grunts. Then he bit
off and ate a small piece, then another small bite, and eventually
taking what was left in his mouth, he finished eating it. After that he
always expected me to stay a minute and speak to him when on
such occasions I gave him an apple. But he never ate it greedily; he
appeared more inclined to talk than to eat, until by degrees I came to
understand what he was saying. What he said was that he appreciated
my kind intentions in giving him apples....So I scratched him
vigorously with my stick, and made him wiggle his body and wink and
blink and smile delightedly all over his face....

I have a friendly feeling towards pigs generally and consider them
the most intelligent of beasts, not excepting the elephant and the
anthropoid ape—the dog is not to be mentioned in this connection.
I also like his disposition and attitude towards all other creatures,
especially man. He is not suspicious and shrinkingly submissive, like
horses, cattle, and sheep; nor an impudent devil-may-care like the
goat; nor hostile like the goose; nor condescending like the cat; nor
a flattering parasite like the dog. He views us from a totally different,
a sort of democratic, standpoint as fellow-citizens and brothers, and
takes it for granted, or grunted, that we understand his language, and
without servility or insolence he has a natural pleasant camerados-all
or hail-fellow-well-met air with us.

—William Henry Hudson, from *The Book of a Naturalist*

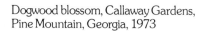
Dogwood blossom, Callaway Gardens,
Pine Mountain, Georgia, 1973

The Dogwood

There is a legend that at the time of the
Crucifixion the dogwood had been the size of
the oak and other forest trees. So firm and
strong was the tree that it was chosen as the
timber for the cross. To be used thus for such
a cruel purpose greatly distressed the tree,
and Jesus, nailed upon it, sensed this, and in
His gentle pity for all sorrow and suffering said
to it: "Because of your regret and pity for My
suffering, never again shall the dogwood tree
grow large enough to be used as a cross.
Henceforth it shall be slender and bent and
twisted and its blossoms shall be in the form of
a cross—two long and two short petals. And
in the center of the outer edge of each petal
there will be nail prints, brown with rust and
stained with red, and in the center of the flower
will be a crown of thorns, and all who see it
will remember."

—Legend, author unknown

Tobacco warehouse, Louisville, Kentucky, date unknown

The Tobacco Market

The men stand wistfully in the road before the tobacco market. Some of them have come to the market alone, others have brought their families. The tobacco farmer rarely has a truck of his own to bring his tobacco to market. "I'm too small a feller for that," he explains. He may own a Model T Ford. You can't haul much tobacco in that.

So he goes in with half a dozen neighbors and they hire a truck to do the hauling—John's tobacco, Jim's, Luther's, Fred's. "A little feller like I am can't put out much, maybe one acre, or two, or three."

"It's really a woman's crop," John says. "You've got to mess and mess with it, all year long." He stands before the warehouse, where the selling is going on. Luther and Jim and Fred stand with him. Fred has had a few shots of moon. You can smell it on him. He keeps slapping Jim on the back and laughing, rather foolishly. He says two of his kids, little fellers, put out half an acre for themselves. He helped them. They are both boys, and one of them wants a bicycle and the other some red-top boots. A man named Love comes up. "Hello, Love," Fred says, and I am a bit startled. "Is that really your name?" I want to ask. Love is built like another Abraham Lincoln. He has a long, scrawny neck, and there are bright red spots on his cheeks. "Look out or tuberculosis will get you," I think. He stands and spits on the ground. He is suspicious of me.

"You ain't a government man, are you?"

—Sherwood Anderson, from "Blue Smoke"
in *Puzzled America*

Cotton field, southern Louisiana, 1964

Those Little Trembling Lodes Which Are the Gins

It is a long tall deep narrow load shored in with weathered wagonsides and bulged up in a high puff above these sides, and the mule, held far over to the right of the highway to let the cars go by, steps more steadily and even more slowly than ordinary, with a look almost of pomp, dragging the hearse-shaped wagon: its iron wheels on the left grince in the slags of the highway, those on the right in clay: and high upon the load, the father at the reins, the whole of the family is sitting, if it is a small family, or if it is a large, those children whose turn it is, and perhaps the mother too. The husband is dressed in the better of his work clothes; the wife, and the children, in such as they might wear to town on saturday, or even, some of them, to church, and the children are happy and excited, high on the soft load, and even a woman is taken with it a little, much more soberly, and even the man who is driving, has in the tightness of his jaws, and in his eyes, which meet those of any stranger with the curious challenging and protective, fearful and fierce pride a poor mother shows when her child, dressed in its best, is being curiously looked at; even he who knows best of any of them, is taken with something of the same: and there is in fact about the whole of it some raw, festal quality, some air also of solemn grandeur, this member in the inconceivably huge and slow parade of mule-drawn, crawling wagons, creaking under the weight of the year's bloodsweated and prayed-over work, on all the roads drawn in, from the utmost runners and ramifications of the slender red roads of all the south and into the southern highways, a wagon every few hundred yards, crested this with a white and this with a black family, all drawn toward those little trembling lodes which are the gins, and all and in each private and silent heart toward that climax of one more year's work which yields so little at best, and nothing so often, and worse to so many hundreds of thousands....

—James Agee, from *Let Us Now Praise Famous Men*

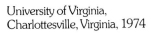
University of Virginia,
Charlottesville, Virginia, 1974

"Freedom of the Human Mind"

I do not have the gift of prophecy, but I know that there is more to be seen ahead than blood upon the face of the moon. There is more to be heard than the rumble of disintegrating cities. What we have created out of man's accumulated knowledge cannot die. There are other visions. I choose gladly to fasten eye and spirit upon these. We can and must believe in the everlastingness of the liberal arts idea, an idea for which a great Virginian once gave immortal definition.

"This institution," said Thomas Jefferson of the University of Virginia, his creation, "will be based on the illimitable freedom of the human mind. For here we are not afraid to follow the truth wherever it may lead, not to tolerate any error so long as reason is left free to combat it."

—Hodding Carter, from *First Person Rural*

Surf seen from lighthouse, Cape Hatteras, North Carolina, 1971

The Shellpicker

This lady, curled like a shell
In her work of love, picks
And pokes at everything. All
The long tide's wilderness
Is grief she touches to tell
How the blazing fish fall
Impossibly down, and the press
Of fathoms under the shell
Pours color up, or locks
The world in a diving bell
As water-shaped and delicate
And full of sound as a shell.
She knows the mysterious, deep
Music that the creatures tell
In rainbows, but in her sleep
The salt sea-weed is all
She catches in her net
Of hands. The fire-fish fall
Up to drown, as tenuous
And insubstantial as the coral
Strikes its flower, or the sun
Prints the smallest shell
With fire, or furious, hacks
Out long lightnings to tell
Its weaving watery shape
Up the Atlantic waves. Small
As any creature in her sleep,
Her hands feed on the shell.
For love she is undone,
And deep as the drowned bell
At death dives to a miracle,
The long sun in her sleep
Becomes a wilderness to tell
The perfect secret of her shape,
This lady, curled like a shell.

—Ronald Perry,
from *Southern Writing in the Sixties/Poetry*

Confederate camp, Warrington Navy Yard,
Pensacola, Florida, 1861

May God Protect Us All

Near Fairfax C.H., Sept. 2nd, 1862

My dear Wife
…My head is well but [a] little more bald than of
yore, a small quantity having been shaved off [by a
Union bullet]. I have certainly been most fortunate
thus far. I have not heard from Willie lately. Gen.
Kearny was killed yesterday. He was one of their
brave Maj. Generals. We marched 42 miles in two
days getting entirely in Pope's rear, taking his
trains, and burning their Depot at Manassas
containing an immense amount of Quartermaster
and commissary stores. Marched [to] Centreville
and…crossed back to the other side of the run,
fought, bled, etc, and in fact performed the most
brilliant and daring feats of Generalship and
soldiership ever performed. The boldness of the
plan and the quickness and completeness of
execution was never beaten. Lee has immortalized
himself and Jackson added new laurels to his
brow—not that I like to be under Jackson, for he
forgets that one ever gets tired, hungry, or sleepy.

   We are resting today but move again tomorrow
morning. We [are] only seven miles from Fairfax
C.H. I have no idea when they will make another
stand. My love to all. May God protect us all and
may we show our gratitude by obeying his laws.

Your devoted Husband

—Wm. Dorsey Pender (C.S.A.) to Fanny Pender,
from *The General to His Lady*

Senator Sam Ervin, Watergate hearings, Washington, D.C., 1973

The Laws of Man and the Laws of God

I can't resist the temptation to philosophize just a little bit about the Watergate.

The evidence thus far introduced or presented before this committee tends to show that men upon whom fortune had smiled benevolently and who possessed great financial power, great political power, and great governmental power, undertook to nullify the laws of man and the laws of God for the purpose of gaining what history will call a very temporary political advantage.

The evidence also indicates that the efforts to nullify the laws of man might have succeeded if it had not been for a courageous Federal judge, Judge Sirica, and a very untiring set of investigative reporters. But you come from a State like the State of Mississippi, where they have great faith in the fact that the laws of God are embodied in the King James version of the Bible, and I think that those who participated in this effort to nullify the laws of man and the laws of God overlooked one of the laws of God which is set forth in the seventh verse of the sixth chapter of Galatians: *Be not deceived. God is not mocked; for whatsoever a man soweth, that shall he also reap.*

— Senator Sam Ervin, before the Select Committee on Presidential Campaign Activities

When We Played We Played It Right

Well, One Eye and Claude would grab that rhythm and hold her by the neck and me and Charley would light out. We'd take that melody and counterpoint and run off with it. Sometimes we would race or do little corkscrew things. Other times we'd go off into the bushes and up into the trees. We'd get ourselves way out. We'd get so far out One Eye and Claude would start worrying and try to bring us back in.

But it would be nice out there and Charley and me knew what we were doing. We didn't even want to come back. And One Eye and Claude would hold on. And it would be me and Charley. The cornet and the trombone. I can still hear it. We'd meet up in the top of those trees and begin chasing each other up one limb and down the other. Finally we'd surprise One Eye and Claude and come charging back down into the melody.

They'd see us coming and there'd be a welcoming committee for us. And then all natural hell would break loose. We'd be bobbing our horns up and down, fast like, like the law was on our tails. And play? Great God Almighty, we played like we were clean out of our minds. And the crowd would be going wild. Doing crazy dances and drinking that liquor like it was Doctor Pepper's. Vicksburg, Hattiesburg, Muscle Shoals…it didn't matter where we played, 'cause when we played we played it right and like it should be played. Man, we played it like we were up on Lake Michigan and playing for Mister Al Capone himself.

—William Price Fox, from "The B-Flat Cornet"
in *Southern Fried Plus Six*

First snow, Blue Ridge Mountains,
Virginia, 1972

A Southern Snow

But the snow itself—there was a beauty about it
few people around here had ever known before.
The snow was not white, as Northerners had
pictured it to be; in the snow there were soft
colors of blue and silver, the sky was a gentle
shining gray. And the dreamy quietness of
falling snow—when had the town been so silent?

People reacted to the snowfall in various
ways. Miss Amelia, on looking out of her window,
thoughtfully wiggled the toes of her bare feet,
gathered close to her neck the collar of her
nightgown. She stood there for some time, then
commenced to draw the shutters and lock every
window on the premises. She closed the place
completely, lighted the lamps, and sat solemnly
over her bowl of grits. The reason for this was not
that Miss Amelia feared the snowfall. It was
simply that she was unable to form an immediate
opinion of this new event, and unless she knew
exactly and definitely what she thought of a
matter (which was nearly always the case) she
preferred to ignore it....

Marvin Macy laid claim to the snowfall. He
said that he knew snow, had seen it in Atlanta,
and from the way he walked about the town that
day it was as though he owned every flake. He
sneered at the little children who crept timidly
out of the houses and scooped up handfuls of
snow to taste. Reverend Willin hurried down the
road with a furious face, as he was thinking
deeply and trying to weave the snow into his
Sunday sermon. Most people were humble and
glad about this marvel; they spoke in hushed
voices and said 'thank you' and 'please' more
than was necessary. A few weak characters, of
course, were demoralized and got drunk—but
they were not numerous. To everyone this was
an occasion and many counted their money and
planned to go to the café that night.

—Carson McCullers, from
The Ballad of the Sad Café and Other Stories

Huey Long, place and date unknown

"They ruled because I put 'em there to rule it"

"You're a lawyer," Hugh Miller said.

"No," the Boss corrected, "I'm not a lawyer. I know some law. In fact, I know a lot of law. And I made me some money out of law. But I'm not a lawyer. That's why I can see what the law is like. It's like a single-bed blanket on a double bed and three folks in the bed and a cold night. There ain't ever enough blanket to cover the case, no matter how much pulling and hauling, and somebody is always going to nigh catch pneumonia. Hell, the law is like the pants you bought last year for a growing boy, but it is always this year and the seams are popped and the shankbone's to the breeze. The law is always too short and too tight for growing humankind. The best you can do is do something and then make up some law to fit and by the time that law gets on the books you would have done something different. Do you think half the things I've done were clear, distinct, and simple in the constitution of this state?"

"The Supreme Court has ruled—" Hugh Miller began.

"Yeah, and they ruled because I put 'em there to rule it, and they saw what had to be done. Half the things weren't in the constitution but they are now, by God. And how did they get there? Simply because somebody did 'em."

—Robert Penn Warren, from *All the King's Men*

Church of St. Thomas,
Barataria, Louisiana, 1945

At a Country Funeral

Now the old ways that have brought us
farther than we remember sink out of sight
as under the treading of many strangers
ignorant of landmarks. Only once in a while
they are cast clear again upon the mind
as at a country funeral where, amid the soft
lights and hothouse flowers, the expensive
solemnity of experts, notes of a polite musician,
persist the usages of old neighborhood.
Friends and kinsmen come and stand and speak,
knowing the extremity they have come to,
one of their own bearing to the earth the last
of his light, his darkness the sun's definitive mark.
They stand and think as they stood and thought
when even the gods were different.
And the organ music, though decorous
as for somebody else's grief, has its source
in the outcry of pain and hope in log churches,
and on naked hillsides by the open grave,
eastward in mountain passes, in tidelands,
and across the sea. How long a time?
Rock of Ages, cleft for me, let me hide my
self in Thee. They came, once in time,
in simple loyalty to their dead, and returned
to the world. The fields and the work
remained to be returned to. Now the entrance
of one of the old ones into the Rock
too often means a lifework perished from the land
without inheritor, and the field goes wild

and the house sits and stares. Or it passes
at cash value into the hands of strangers.
Now the old dead wait in the open coffin
for the blood kin to gather, come home
for one last time, to hear old men
whose tongues bear an essential topography
speak memories doomed to die.
But our memory of ourselves, hard earned,
is one of the land's seeds, as a seed
is the memory of the life of its kind in its place,
to pass on into life the knowledge
of what has died. What we owe the future
is not a new start, for we can only begin
with what has happened. We owe the future
the past, the long knowledge
that is the potency of time to come.
That makes of a man's grave a rich furrow.
The community of knowing in common is the seed
of our life in this place. There is not only
no better possibility, there is no
other, except for chaos and darkness,
the terrible ground of the only possible
new start. And so as the old die and the young
depart, where shall a man go who keeps
the memories of the dead, except home
again, as one would go back after a burial,
faithful to the fields, lest the dead die
a second and more final death.

—Wendell Berry, from *The Country of Marriage*

Seabreeze, Florida, circa 1900

roBUST and HYPnotic

Dear Cousin,

I am snatching a few moments from the daily rush to again urge you to join Me.…With the idea of enticing you, I will attempt to give a fleeting glimpse of the passing show.

During the bathing hours at high tide…the beach and hotel verandas are crowded with onlookers. An hundred or more bathers —men and women—afford us no end of entertainment. Charlie Dudley is here and, as you know, one permits him to say outrageous things. The combination of his charm and daring humor are disarming. He sat beside me today while all eyes were riveted on one Mrs. Gissing from Chicago. She is supposed to be beautiful. I make a guess that her auburn tresses have been assisted and her figure is described by Charlie as being roBUST and HYPnotic. Some say, "divorcee," others "grass-widow." Well, no matter. In any case it would take a horse race to keep up with her. I, of course, know her only by sight, and *sight* she is! The men buzz around her like bees and gather about the bath rooms to see her pass, en route to the waves. She always lolls on the sand a bit before making a kittenish dash— she's surely in the thirties if a minute. Her costume and antics this morning were paramount to anything yet. ("Yet" is significant as there is no telling what she may do.)

Black silk bathing suit—*very* short skirt—*very* low neck NO sleeves —transparent silk stockings. On her arm a gold bracelet, if you please! After she had done building sand hills (childish aspect) with several male bathers, she referred to the billows. Catching hands with a favored gentleman, they made a grand rush and sprawled. From then on, where her corset began and left off was very apparent.

Mrs. G., with one exception, is the only good female swimmer, yet, with an arm around the man's shoulder, his arm around her's, swimming with one hand apiece, they made good headway to the deep water raft. Not satisfied with this, she mounted his back and pitched off head foremost. Some women seated next to me got up and left. I didn't feel that way about Mrs. Gissing. For all I care she may be as brazen as she likes.

—David L. Cohn, from *The Good Old Days*

Civil War battlefield,
Cold Harbor, Virginia, 1975

Stonewall at Cold Harbor

General Jackson mounted his gaunt sorrel…and leaving his position
moved more to the front. At that moment someone handed him
a lemon—a fruit of which he was specially fond. Immediately a small
piece was bitten out of it and slowly and unsparingly he began to extract
its flavor and its juice. From that moment until darkness ended the
battle, that lemon scarcely left his lips except to be used as a baton to
emphasize an order. He listened to Yankee shout or Rebel yell, to the
sound of musketry advancing or receding, to all the signs of promise
or apprehension, but he never for an instant lost his interest in that
lemon and even spoke of its excellence. His face, nevertheless, was
calm and granite-like. His blue eye was restful and cold, except when
now and then it gave, for a moment, an ominous flash. His right hand
lay open and flat on his thigh, but now and then was raised into the air
as was his habit—a gesture which the troops learned to believe was as
significant as the extended arm of Aaron. But the lemon was not
abandoned.

The moment came when it was taken from his mouth with an
impatient jerk. A wild yell came from the battlefield which attracted his
attention. Pendleton came up and said it was from the Stonewall
Brigade, for he had just seen Winder taking them in. He drew the
lemon away abruptly and said, "We shall soon have good news from
that charge. Yes, they are driving the enemy!" and he lifted up his
yellow banner, as if in triumph. When I last saw that lemon, it was torn
open and exhausted and thrown away, but the day was over and the
battle was won.

H. K. Douglas, from *I Rode With Stonewall*

Saturday afternoon, courthouse square,
Williamsburg, Kentucky, 1950

In the Square

Maycomb was an old town, but it was a
tired old town when I first knew it. In rainy
weather the streets turned to red slop;
grass grew on the sidewalks, the courthouse sagged in the square. Somehow,
it was hotter then: a black dog suffered on
a summer's day; bony mules hitched to
Hoover carts flicked flies in the sweltering
shade of the live oaks on the square.
Men's stiff collars wilted by nine in the
morning. Ladies bathed before noon,
after their three-o'clock naps, and by
nightfall were like soft teacakes with
frostings of sweat and sweet talcum.

　　People moved slowly then. They
ambled across the square, shuffled in and
out of the stores around it, took their
time about everything. A day was twenty-
four hours long but seemed longer. There
was no hurry, for there was nowhere to
go, nothing to buy and no money to buy
it with, nothing to see outside the
boundaries of Maycomb County. But it
was a time of vague optimism for some
of the people: Maycomb County had
recently been told that it had nothing to
fear but fear itself.

—Harper Lee, from
To Kill a Mockingbird

Lone grave, Big Bend National Park, Texas, 1970

The Spirit of This Plot of Earth

What is the spirit, the tempo, the rhythm of this plot of earth to which we belong…? Often it seems that the essential spirit has been run over and killed. But nature is as inexorable, as passionless, and as patient in revenge as she is in fidelity to "the heart that loves her." In the long run, she cannot be betrayed by man; in the long run, man can betray only himself by not harmonizing with her.

> —J. Frank Dobie,
> from "The Writer and His Region"
> in *Southwest Review,* Spring, 1950

Appalachian family, Reems Creek,
near Asheville, North Carolina, 1916

In Every Child

In every child who is born,
under no matter what circumstances,
and of no matter what parents,
the potentiality of the human race
is born again: and in him, too,
once more, and of each of us,
our terrific responsibility towards
human life; towards the utmost idea of
goodness, of the horror of error,
and of God.

—James Agee, from *Let Us Now
Praise Famous Men*

The Apalachee River, near Madison, Georgia, 1974

Inside the River

Dark, deeply. A red.
All levels moving
A given surface.
Break this. Step down.
Follow your right
Foot nakedly in
To another body.
Put on the river
Like a fleeing coat,
A garment of motion,
Tremendous, immortal.
Find a still root

To hold you in it.
Let flowing create
A new, inner being:
As the source in the mountain
Gives water in pulses,
These can be felt at
The heart of the current.
And here it is only
One wandering step
Forth, to the sea.
Your freed hair floating
Out of your brain,

Wait for a coming
And swimming idea.
Live like the dead
In their flying feeling.
Loom as a ghost
When life pours through it.
Crouch in the secret
Released underground
With the earth of the fields
All around you, gone
Into purposeful grains
That stream like dust

In a holy hallway.
Weight more changed
Than that of one
Now being born,
Let go the root.
Move with the world
As the deep dead move,
Opposed to nothing.
Release. Enter the sea
Like a winding wind.
No. Rise. Draw breath.
Sing. See no one.

—James Dickey, from *Drowning with Others*

For the Dignity of Man

I speak tonight for the dignity of man and the destiny of democracy....At times history and fate meet at a single time in a single place to shape a turning point in man's unending search for freedom. So it was at Lexington and Concord. So it was a century ago at Appomattox. So it was last week in Selma, Alabama.

   There is no constitutional issue here. The command of the Constitution is plain. There is no moral issue. It is wrong—deadly wrong—to deny any of your fellow Americans the right to vote in this country. There is no issue of states' rights or national rights. There is only the struggle for human rights.... This time, on this issue, there must be no delay, no hesitation, and no compromise with our purpose.

   But even if we pass this bill, the battle will not be over. What happened in Selma is part of a far larger movement which reaches into every section and state of America. It is the effort of American Negroes to secure for themselves the full blessings of American life.

   Their cause must be our cause too. Because it is not just Negroes, but really it is all of us who must overcome the crippling legacy of bigotry and injustice. And...we...shall...overcome.

—President Lyndon Baines Johnson,
from a speech before the U.S. Congress, March 15, 1965

Civil rights marchers on the road to
Montgomery, Alabama, 1965

Clinchfield Engine #1,
Hawkins County, Tennessee, 1973

In the Great Train

Toward midnight there is another pause at a
larger town—the last stop in Catawba—again
the feeling of wild unrest and nameless joy and
sorrow. The traveller gets out, walks up and
down the platform, sees the vast slow flare and
steaming of the mighty engine, rushes into the
station, and looks into the faces of all the people
passing with the same sense of instant familiarity,
greeting, and farewell—that lonely, strange, and
poignantly wordless feeling that Americans
know so well. Then he is in the pullman again,
the last outposts of the town have slipped away
from him and the great train which all through
the afternoon has travelled eastward from the
mountains half across the mighty State, is now
for the first time pointed northward, worldward,
towards the secret borders of Virginia, towards
the great world cities of his hope, the fable of his
childhood legendry, and the wild and secret
hunger of his heart, his spirit and his life.

Already the little town from which he came in
the great hills, the faces of his kinsmen and his
friends, their most familiar voices, the shapes of
things he knew seem far and strange as dreams,
lost at the bottom of the million-visaged
sea-depth of dark time, the strange and bitter
miracle of life. He cannot think that he has ever
lived there in the far lost hills, or ever left them,
and all his life seems stranger than the dream of
time, and the great train moves on across the
immense and lonely visage of America, making
its great monotone that is the sound of silence
and forever. And in the train, and in ten
thousand little towns, the sleepers sleep upon
the earth.

—Thomas Wolfe, from *Of Time and the River*

Basic training, Fort Benning,
Georgia, 1940

"Come out in the sunshine, kiddies!"

Dear, unfortunate civilian friend:

I am very enthusiastic about Army life. We lie around in bed every morning until at least six o'clock. This, of course, gives us plenty of time to get washed and dressed and make the bunks, etc., by 6:10. At 6:15 we stand outside and shiver while some (deleted) blows a bugle. After we are reasonably chilled, we grope our way through the darkness to the mess hall. Here we have a hearty breakfast consisting of an unidentified liquid and a choice of white or rye crusts.

After gorging ourselves with this delicious repast, we waddle our way back to the barracks. We have nothing to do until 7:30 so we just sit around and scrub toilets, mop the floors, wash the windows and pick up all the matchsticks and cigarette butts within a radius of 2,000 feet of the barracks.

Soon the sergeant comes in and says, "Come out in the sunshine, kiddies!" So we go out and bask in the wonderful North Carolina sunshine—of course, we stand knee-deep in the wonderful North Carolina sand. To limber up, we do a few simple calisthenics, such as touching your toes with both feet off the ground and grabbing yourself by the hair and holding yourself at arm's length....

—Marion Hargrove, from *See Here, Private Hargrove*

A Worn Path

It was December—a bright frozen day in the early morning. Far out in the country there was an old Negro woman with her head tied in a red rag, coming along a path through the pinewoods. Her name was Phoenix Jackson. She was very old and small and she walked slowly in the dark pine shadows, moving a little from side to side in her steps, with the balanced heaviness and lightness of a pendulum in a grandfather clock. She carried a thin, small cane made from an umbrella, and with this she kept tapping the frozen earth in front of her. This made a grave and persistent noise in the still air, that seemed meditative, like the chirping of a solitary little bird.

She wore a dark striped dress reaching down to her shoetops, and an equally long apron of bleached sugar sacks, with a full pocket; all neat and tidy, but every time she took a step she might have fallen over her shoelaces, which dragged from her unlaced shoes. She looked straight ahead. Her eyes were blue with age. Her skin had a pattern all its own of numberless branching wrinkles and as though a whole little tree stood in the middle of her forehead, but a golden color ran underneath, and the two knobs of her cheeks were illuminated by a yellow burning under the dark. Under the red rag her hair came down on her neck in the frailest of ringlets, still black, and with an odor like copper.

Now and then there was a quivering in the thicket. Old Phoenix said, "Out of my way, all you foxes, owls, beetles, jack rabbits, coons, and wild animals....Keep out from under these feet, little bobwhites....Keep the big wild hogs out of my path. Don't let none of those come running my direction. I got a long way." Under her small black-freckled hand her cane, limber as a buggy whip, would switch at the brush as if to rouse up any hiding things.

On she went. The woods were deep and still. The sun made the pine needles almost too bright to look at, up where the wind rocked. The cones dropped as light as feathers. Down in the hollow was the mourning dove—it was not too late for him.

The path ran up a hill. "Seem like there is chains about my feet, time I get this far," she said, in the voice of argument old people keep to use with themselves. "Something always take a hold on this hill—pleads I should stay."

After she got to the top she turned and gave a full, severe look behind her where she had come. "Up through pines," she said at length. "Now down through oaks."

Her eyes opened their widest and she started down gently. But before she got to the bottom of the hill a bush caught her dress.

Her fingers were busy and intent, but her skirts were full and long, so that before she could pull them free in one place they were caught in another. It was not possible to allow the dress to tear. "I in the thorny bush," she said. "Thorns, you doing your appointed work. Never want to let folks past—no sir. Old eyes thought you was a pretty little *green* bush."

Finally, trembling all over, she stood free, and after a moment dared to stoop for her cane.

"Sun so high!" she cried, leaning back and looking, while the thick tears went over her eyes. "The time getting all gone here."

At the foot of this hill was a place where a log was laid across the creek.

"Now comes the trial," said Phoenix.

Putting her right foot out, she mounted the log and shut her eyes. Lifting her skirt, leveling her cane fiercely before her, like a festival figure in some parade, she began to march across. Then she opened her eyes and she was safe on the other side.

"I wasn't as old as I thought," she said.

—Eudora Welty, from *A Curtain of Green and Other Stories*

Chet Atkins in concert,
Chattanooga, Tennessee, 1975

The End of the Rainbow

If you were raised some 20 years ago in a place like Hamilton, Ala., or Norman, Okla., or Hazard, Ky., your Saturday nights took on a definite pattern. Once the chores were done and night began to close in, the entire family would huddle around the big Zenith radio in the living room and the old man would start hunting for 650 on the dial, for clear-channel WSM, "the broadcasting service of the National Life and Accident Insurance Company, Nashville, Tennessee," for the Grand Old Opry. Then, until midnight, weary legs and cracked hands and broken spirits would be resurrected by the familiar sounds crackling over the radio: Ernest Tubb's bullfrog voice singing "Walkin' the Floor Over You," and Hank Williams yodeling his "Lovesick Blues," and Roy Acuff wailing "Great Speckled Bird" as silvery ribbons of tears streamed down his deep-ridged face, and the crowd at Ryman Auditorium in Nashville whooping at the absurdity of Cousin Minnie Pearl, in that store-bought hat with the price tag still dangling, giving out the latest gossip from her make-believe town (or was it?), Grinder's Switch. The Opry leaves an indelible scar on your heart when you have let it be that big a part of your young life, like the mark left by your mother's love, and a dream that won't let you go is the dream of one day going to Nashville and entering the same old auditorium and sitting through a whole night of the Opry. The dream is even more important, of course, to those who learn how to pick a guitar or sing. A country boy with a guitar dreams of playing on the stage of the Opry just as fervently as a kid with a baseball bat dreams of one day stepping into the batter's box at Yankee Stadium. The Opry is country music's Yankee Stadium and Carnegie Hall and White House. "The Opry," says General Manager Bud Wendell, "is the end of the rainbow."

—Paul Hemphill, from *The Nashville Sound: Bright Lights and Country Music*

Turkey shoot, Dothan, Alabama, circa 1930

Hunters

In September the dove shoot at Oman Hedgepath's farm, hunters surrounding the fields at midday, the sounds of shooting, pink and gray feathers of the mourning doves settling into the corn stubble; the bright colors of empty shot shell hulls littering the ground, and above this, the plaintive whimper of the feeding call, birds slicing and dodging through the clean dry air; Negroes gathering the stiff, feather-soft bodies and cleaning them, keeping only the burgundy-colored, heart-shaped breasts.

November opened bird season—bobwhite quail. Southeast then to plantation on the Alabama line. They rode to the coveys on horseback, making a gallery of the same ladies and gentlemen who opened the dove season at Oman's farm—the best lawyers, the big landowners, the state senators, the crack surgeons, the bank presidents and their hard, graceful women. For three long days they rode, dismounting only to shoot over the quivering backs of the Brittany spaniels, dogs trained and hardened through the summer in Canada. The dog handlers went quickly ahead on foot, like Indians; behind the riders came the Negro grooms, running up to hold horses when the hunters dismounted.

—Jesse Hill Ford, from *The Liberation of Lord Byron Jones*

Prisoners, Ellis, Texas, 1969

Twelve Mortal Men

The Forks Falls highway is three miles from the town, and it is here the chain gang has been working. The road is of macadam, and the county decided to patch up the rough places and widen it at a certain dangerous place. The gang is made up of twelve men, all wearing black and white striped prison suits, and chained at the ankles. There is a guard, with a gun, his eyes drawn to red slits by the glare. The gang works all the day long, arriving huddled in the prison cart soon after daybreak, and being driven off again in the gray August twilight. All day there is the sound of the picks striking into the clay earth, hard sunlight, the smell of sweat. And every day there is music. One dark voice will start a phrase, half-sung, and like a question. And after a moment another voice will join in, soon the whole gang will be singing. The voices are dark in the golden glare, the music intricately blended, both somber and joyful. The music will swell until at last it seems that the sound does not come from the twelve men on the gang, but from the earth itself, or the wide sky. It is music that causes the heart to broaden and the listener to grow cold with ecstasy and fright. Then slowly the music will sink down until at last there remains one lonely voice, then a great hoarse breath, the sun, the sound of the picks in the silence.

And what kind of gang is this that can make such music? Just twelve mortal men, seven of them black and five of them white boys from this county. Just twelve mortal men who are together.

—Carson McCullers, from
The Ballad of the Sad Café and Other Stories

And None Can Care, Beyond That Room

Above that shell and carapace, more frail against heaven than fragilest membrane of glass, nothing, straight to the terrific stars: whereof all heaven is chalky; and of whom the nearest is so wild a reach my substance wilts to think on: and we…are seated among these stars alone: none to turn to, none to make us known; a little country settlement so deep, so lost in shelve and shade of dew, no one so much as laughs at us. Small wonder how pitiably we love our home, cling in her skirts at night, rejoice in her wide star-seducing smile, when every star strikes us sick with the fright: do we really exist at all?

> This world is not my home, I'm, only passing through,
> My treasures and my hopes, are, all, beyond the sky,
> I've many, friends, and kindreds, that's gone, along before,
> And I can't, feel, at home, in this world, any, more.

And thus, too, these families, not otherwise than with every family in the earth, how each, apart, how inconceivably lonely, sorrowful, and remote! Not one other on earth, nor in any dream, that can care so much what comes to them, so that even as they sit at the lamp and eat their supper, the joke they are laughing at could not be so funny to anyone else; and the littlest child who stands on the bench solemnly, with food glittering all over his cheeks in the lamplight, this littlest child I speak of is not there, he is of another family, and it is a different woman who wipes the food from his cheeks and takes his weight upon her thighs and against her body and who feeds him, and lets his weight slacken against her in his heavying sleep;…and the people next up the road cannot care in the same way, not for any of it: for they are absorbed upon themselves: and the negroes down beyond the spring have drawn their shutters tight, the lamplight pulses like wounded honey through the seams into the soft night, and there is laughter: but nobody else cares. All over the whole round earth and in the settlements, the towns, and the great iron stones of cities, people are drawn inward within their little shells of rooms, and are to be seen in their wondrous and pitiful actions through the surfaces of their lighted windows by thousands, by millions, little golden aquariums, in chairs, reading, setting tables, sewing, playing cards, not talking, talking, laughing inaudibly, mixing drinks, at radio dials, eating, in shirt-sleeves, carefully dressed, courting, teasing, loving, seducing, undressing, leaving the room empty in its empty light, alone and writing a letter urgently, in couples married, in separate chairs, in family parties, in gay parties, preparing for bed, preparing for sleep: and none can care, beyond that room….

— James Agee, from *Let Us Now Praise Famous Men*

With This Faith

This afternoon I have a dream. It is a dream deeply rooted in the American dream. I have
a dream that one day right down in Georgia and Mississippi and Alabama the sons of former
slaves and the sons of former slave owners will be able to live together as brothers....

I have a dream this afternoon that one day men will no longer burn down houses and the
church of God simply because people want to be free. I have a dream this afternoon that
there will be a day...when all men can live with dignity...that my four little children will not
come up in the same young days that I came up in—that they will be judged on the basis of
the content of their character, not the color of their skin....

I have a dream this afternoon that one day in this land the words of Amos will become real.
And justice will roll down like waters and righteousness like a mighty stream....

I have a dream this afternoon that one day everybody will be exalted—every hill and valley
shall be made low—the rough places will be made plain and the crooked places will be made
straight and the glory of the Lord shall be revealed and all flesh shall see it together.

I have a dream this afternoon that the brotherhood of man will become a reality in this day.
With this faith I will go out to carve a tunnel of hope through the mountain of despair. With
this faith I will go out with you and transform dark yesterdays into bright tomorrows. With
this faith we will be able to achieve this new day when all of God's children—black men and
white men, Jews and Gentiles, Protestants and Catholics—will be able to join hands and
sing with the Negro in the spiritual of old, 'Free at last, free at last! Thank God Almighty,
we're free at last.'

—Rev. Martin Luther King, Jr., from "I Have a Dream"

Lynchburg YMCA camp,
George Washington National Forest, Virginia, 1936

The Swimmers

SCENE: *Montgomery County,
          Kentucky, July 1911*

Kentucky water, clear springs: a boy fleeing
  To water under the dry Kentucky sun,
  His four little friends in tandem with him, seeing

Long shadows of grapevine wriggle and run
  Over the green swirl; mullein under the ear
  Soft as Nausicaä's palm; sullen fun

Savage as childhood's thin harmonious tear:
  O fountain, bosom source undying-dead
  Replenish me the spring of love and fear

And give me back the eye that looked and fled
  When a thrush idling in the tulip tree
  Unwound the cold dream of the copperhead.

—Along the creek the road was winding; we
  Felt the quicksilver sky. I see again
  The shrill companions of that odyssey:

Bill Eaton, Charlie Watson, 'Nigger' Layne
  The doctor's son, Harry Duesler who played
  The flute; and Tate, with water on the brain.

Dog-days: the dusty leaves where rain delayed
  Hung low on poison-oak and scuppernong,
  And we were following the active shade

Of water, that bells and bickers all night long....

—Allen Tate, from *The Swimmers
and Other Selected Poems*

Mule team in meadow, Holly Creek, Kentucky, 1973

For the Chance to Kick You Once

A mule which will gallop for a half-mile in the single direction elected by its rider even one time becomes a neighborhood legend; one that will do it consistently time after time is an incredible phenomenon. Because, unlike a horse, a mule is far too intelligent to break its heart for glory running around the rim of a mile-long saucer. In fact, I rate mules second only to rats in intelligence, the mule followed in order by cats, dogs, and horses last—assuming of course that you accept my definition of intelligence: which is the ability to cope with environment: which means to accept environment yet still retain at least something of personal liberty.

The rat of course I rate first. He lives in your house without helping you to buy it or build it or repair it or keep the taxes paid; he eats what you eat without helping you raise it or buy it or even haul it into the house; you cannot get rid of him; were he not a cannibal, he would long since have inherited the earth. The cat is third, with some of the same qualities but a weaker, punier creature; he neither toils nor spins, he is a parasite on you but he does not love you; he would die, cease to exist, vanish from the earth (I mean, in his so-called domestic form) but so far he has not had to. (There is the fable, Chinese I think, literary I am sure: of a period on earth when the dominant creatures were cats: who after ages of trying to cope with the anguishes of mortality—famine, plague, war, injustice, folly, greed—in a word, civilised government—convened a congress of the wisest cat philosophers to see if anything could be done: who after long deliberation agreed that the dilemma, the problems themselves were insoluble and the only practical solution was to give it up, relinquish, abdicate, by selecting from among the lesser creatures a species, race optimistic enough to believe that the mortal predicament could be solved and ignorant enough never to learn better. Which is why the cat lives with you, is completely dependent on you for food and shelter but lifts no paw for you and loves you not; in a word, why your cat looks at you the way it does.)

The dog I rate fourth. He is courageous, faithful, monogamous in his devotion; he is your parasite too: his failure (as compared to the cat) is that he will work for you—I mean, willingly, gladly, ape any trick, no matter how silly, just to please you, for a pat on the head....
The horse I rate last. A creature capable of but one idea at a time, his strongest quality is timidity and fear. He can be tricked and cajoled by a child into breaking his limbs or his heart too in running too far too fast or jumping things too wide or hard or high; he will eat himself to death if not guarded like a baby; if he had only one gram of the intelligence of the most backward rat, he would be the rider.

The mule I rate second. But second only because you can make him work for you. But that too only within his own rigid self-set regulations. He will not permit himself to eat too much. He will draw a wagon or a plow, but he will not run a race. He will not try to jump anything he does not indubitably know before-hand he can jump; he will not enter any place unless he knows of his own knowledge what is on the other side; he will work for you patiently for ten years for the chance to kick you once. In a word, free of the obligations of ancestry and the responsibilities of posterity, he has con-quered not only life but death too and hence is immortal; were he to vanish from the earth today, the same chanceful biological combination which produced him yesterday would produce him a thousand years hence, unaltered, unchanged, incorrigible still within the limitations which he himself had proved and tested; still free, still coping. Which is why Ned's mule was unique, a phenomenon. Put a dozen mules on a track and when the word Go is given, a dozen different directions will be taken, like a scattering of disturbed bugs on the surface of a pond; the one of the twelve whose direction happens to coincide with the track, will inevitably win.

—William Faulkner, from *The Reivers*

Due West Plantation,
Tallahatchie County, Mississippi, 1968

"The True Test of Civilization"

The conclusion of the whole matter is that the final goal of agricultural progress is simply the development of a richer and finer rural civilization and rural culture, and all other reforms or attempts at improvements are steps or means to this end. Emerson said: "The true test of civilization is not the census, nor the size of cities, nor crops; no, but the kind of men the country turns out." And this is just the thought which Dr. Carver once expressed in its agricultural implications when he said in a letter to the writer: "The final test of good agriculture is the growing of good men and women who are thoroughbreds in the real sense of the word."

This is indeed the ultimate goal of agricultural progress. We must recognize the fact that the real farm problem is not one problem but a variety of problems linked together, all looking to one result, namely, the development of a richer and more satisfying rural civilization.

—Clarence Poe, from *Farm Life:
Problems and Opportunities*

Four generations,
Louisville, Kentucky, 1920

What It Is to Love

We are speaking of love. A leaf, a handful of seed—
begin with these, learn a little what it is to love. First,
a leaf, a fall of rain, then someone to receive what a leaf
has taught you, what a fall of rain has ripened. No easy
process, understand; it could take a lifetime, it has mine,
and still I've never mastered it—I only know how true it
is: that love is a chain of love, as nature is a chain of life.

—Truman Capote, from *The Grass Harp*

Photo Information

Willie Morris and his son David, near Yazoo City, Mississippi, 1967; photograph by Hans Namuth

William Faulkner, Lafayette County, Mississippi, 1962; photograph by Martin Dain—Magnum

Fiddler, Reuben, Arkansas, 1968; photograph by Dan J. McCoy—Black Star

General store, Moundville, Alabama, 1936; photograph by Walker Evans—Library of Congress

Robert E. Lee monument, Richmond, Virginia, 1974; photograph by David White—Black Star

Country road, eastern Kentucky, 1973; photograph by Margaret MacKichan

Start of Daytona 400, Daytona Beach, Florida, 1974; photograph by Don Hunter

The Outer Banks, Avon, North Carolina, 1975; photograph by Gerald Crawford—*Southern Living*

Oklahoma cheerleaders, Texas-Oklahoma football game, Dallas, Texas, 1958; photograph by Marvin E. Newman

Will Rogers, place and date unknown; Culver Pictures

Chrétien Point Plantation, Sunset, Louisiana, 1946; photograph by Clarence John Laughlin, © 1962

Wedding group, White Sulphur Springs, West Virginia, circa 1900; Atlanta Historical Society

World première, *Gone With The Wind*, Atlanta, Georgia, 1939; UPI

Lyndon Johnson and other elementary school teachers, Cotulla, Texas, 1928; Wide World

Tallulah Bankhead with her father and stepmother, place and date unknown; Culver Pictures

Cowboys on trail in the Southwest, 1967; photograph by Burk Uzzle—Magnum

River baptism near Richmond, Virginia, 1896; Cook Collection, Valentine Museum, Richmond

Clarence Darrow at Scopes trial, Dayton, Tennessee, 1925; Culver Pictures

Coon dogs, Renfroe Valley, Kentucky, 1975; photograph by Gerald Crawford—*Southern Living*

Cotton day, Prairie Street, Eutaw, Alabama, October 14, 1893; University of Alabama

Alabama classroom, circa 1920; University of Alabama

Wagon wheels, Madison, Georgia, 1974; photograph by William A. Bake

Ty Cobb stealing third base, place and date unknown; Culver Pictures

Deer in Everglades Park, Florida, 1971; photograph by Fred Ward—Black Star

Tenant farmers, Eutaw, Alabama, 1937; photograph by Dorothea Lange for the FSA—Library of Congress

Dry Run Christian Church, Shenandoah Valley, Virginia, 1973; photograph by James R. Smith

Mallards in flight, Atlantic flyway, 1968; photograph by Tony Florio—National Audubon Society

The first Coca-Cola truck in Knoxville, Tennessee, 1909; The Coca-Cola Company, Atlanta

Ku Klux Klan, Mississippi, 1964; photograph by Bruce Roberts—Photo Researchers

Bobby Jones on the first fairway at Pebble Beach, California, 1929. Note cigarette. UPI

Caretaker among Union tombstones at Andersonville, Georgia, 1970; photograph by Al Clayton

Fisherman, Okeefenokee Swamp, Georgia, 1959; photograph by Tom Hollyman—Photo Researchers

Dogwood blossom, Callaway Gardens, Pine Mountain, Georgia, 1973; photograph by Gerald Crawford—*Southern Living*

Tobacco warehouse, Louisville, Kentucky, date unknown; Caulfield & Shook Collection, University of Louisville

Cotton field, southern Louisiana, 1964; photograph by Charles Harbutt—Magnum

Franklin Roosevelt fishing at Warm Springs, Georgia, 1930; Franklin Roosevelt Library

Shrimp boat, off Morehead City, North Carolina, 1968; photograph by Bruce Roberts—Photo Researchers

Evergreen Plantation, West Mississippi River Road, Louisiana, 1947; photograph by Clarence John Laughlin, © 1973

The *Mary S. Blees* on the Tombigbee River, Murphy's Bluff, Alabama, date unknown; University of Alabama

Hundredth running of the Kentucky Derby, Louisville, 1974; Richard Nugent—Louisville *Courier-Journal*

Hampton Institute, Virginia, 1899; photograph by Frances B. Johnston—Museum of Modern Art

Moonshine still, West Virginia, 1934 (note NRA scrawled on barrel); Culver Pictures

World War I soldiers marching down street in Louisville, Kentucky, date unknown

"By the Chinaberry Tree," Tifton, Georgia, 1938; photograph by Dorothea Lange for the FSA—The Oakland Museum

Colonnade at the University of Virginia, Charlottesville, Virginia, 1974; photograph by David Morris

Surf seen from lighthouse, Cape Hatteras, North Carolina, 1971; photograph by Frank J. Miller—Photo Researchers

Confederate camp, Warrington Navy Yard, Pensacola, Florida, 1861; The Bettmann Archive

Senator Sam Ervin of North Carolina at the Watergate hearings in Washington, D.C., 1973; photograph by Sven Simon

Olympia Brass Marching Band, New Orleans, Louisiana, 1973; photograph by John Donnels

First snow, Blue Ridge Mountains, Virginia, 1972; photograph by Tony Castelvecchi—Black Star

Civil War battlefield, Cold Harbor, Virginia, 1975; photograph by William A. Bake

Saturday afternoon, courthouse square, Williamsburg, Kentucky, 1950; photograph by Barney Cowherd

Lone grave, Big Bend National Park, Texas, 1970; photograph by Gerald Crawford—*Southern Living*

Clinchfield Engine #1, Hawkins County, Tennessee, 1973; photograph by Earl Carter

Calisthenics during basic training at Fort Benning, Georgia, 1940; Wide World

Pine thicket, Tucker, Georgia, 1974; photograph by William A. Bake

Cabin, Great Smoky Mountains, 1971; photograph by Dan J. McCoy— Black Star

Medical students, University of Alabama in Birmingham, 1975; photograph by Gerald Crawford—*Southern Living*

Lynchburg YMCA camp, George Washington National Forest, Virginia, 1936; U.S. Forest Service

Huey Long of Louisiana, place and date unknown; a still from "The March of Time" — Culver Pictures

Church of St. Thomas, Barataria, Louisiana, 1945; photograph by Edwin Russkam, University of Louisville

Seabreeze, Florida, now part of Daytona Beach, circa 1900; Library of Congress

Appalachian family, Reems Creek, near Asheville, North Carolina, 1916; photograph by William A. Barnhill

The Apalachee River, near Madison, Georgia, 1974; photograph by William A. Bake

Civil rights marchers on the road to Montgomery, Alabama, 1965; photograph by Matt Herron — Black Star

Chet Atkins in concert, Chattanooga, Tennessee, 1975; photograph by Gerald Crawford — *Southern Living*

Turkey shoot, Dothan, Alabama, circa 1930; University of Alabama

Prisoners, Ellis, Texas, 1969; photograph by Danny Lyon — Magnum

Mule team in meadow, Holly Creek, Kentucky, 1973; photograph by Margaret MacKichan

Due West Plantation, Tallahatchie County, Mississippi, 1968; photograph by Bob Adelman

Four generations of a Louisville family; Caulfield & Shook Collection, University of Louisville

A Southern Album

Designed by The Glusker Group, Inc., New York City.

Text composed in Alphatype Souvenir by Quad Typographers, Inc., New York City.

Color-separation photography and film prepared by Graphic Arts Corporation of Ohio, Toledo, Ohio.